HOW TO TALK
TO YOUR DOG

HOW TO TALK TO YOUR DOG

You and Your Dog Will Be
Happier Once You Learn How
to Understand Each Other!

CON SLOBODCHIKOFF

LYONS
PRESS

Essex, Connecticut

An imprint of Globe Pequot, the trade division of
The Rowman & Littlefield Publishing Group, Inc.
4501 Forbes Blvd., Ste. 200
Lanham, MD 20706
www.rowman.com

Distributed by NATIONAL BOOK NETWORK

British Library Cataloguing in Publication Information Available

Library of Congress Cataloging-in-Publication Data

Names: Slobodchikoff, C. N., author.
Title: How to talk to your dog : you and your dog will be happier once you
  learn how to understand each other! / Con Slobodchikoff.
Description: Essex, Connecticut : Lyons Press, [2024] | Includes
  bibliographical references and index.
Identifiers: LCCN 2024006470 (print) | LCCN 2024006471 (ebook) | ISBN
  9781493085064 (trade paperback) | ISBN 9781493085071 (epub)
Subjects: LCSH: Dogs—Behavior. | Dogs—Psychology. | Human-animal
  relationships.
Classification: LCC SF433 .S595 2024 (print) | LCC SF433 (ebook) | DDC
  636.7/0887—dc23/eng/20240423
LC record available at https://lccn.loc.gov/2024006470
LC ebook record available at https://lccn.loc.gov/2024006471

∞™ The paper used in this publication meets the minimum requirements of
American National Standard for Information Sciences—Permanence of Paper
for Printed Library Materials, ANSI/NISO Z39.48-1992.

CONTENTS

1

DOGS HAVE LANGUAGE

In this book, I'll lead you on a journey of how you can start talking to your dog. Once you learn how to do that, both you and your dog will be much happier knowing that each can understand the other.

Would you like to talk to your dog? To have a deep connection? To feel that you and your dog are really communicating? Some people say this is a fantasy. They say that dogs don't understand human language. That they only understand the tone of voice. That they're dumb brutes who are lovable and cuddly, but not very bright. That they can't think, they can't plan, and they barely remember things from day to day. And, according to these people, dogs certainly don't have their own language.

Do you believe that dogs have language and can talk? I do. I have looked extensively at animal languages and have concluded that a number of animals have their own language. We just need to listen in the right way and respond in a way that is meaningful to the animals.

We need to keep in mind that language is not just spoken words. Language is anything that conveys meaningful information in an organized structured way. Language can involve visual signals, spoken signals, odor signals, or signals through touch. We like to think that our language is exclusively a spoken one. But we send off visual signals and odor signals every time we talk to somebody in person. So it is with dogs.

Luckily for us, dogs are able to learn a number of human words. A border collie named Chaser, who died in 2019, knew 1,022 nouns: the names of 800 cloth animals, 116 balls, 26 frisbees, and a variety of plastic objects. Another border collie, Rico, who died in 2008, knew 200 different words. My two standard poodles, Zephyr and Raja, knew a variety of different words. If I said, "let's go for a walk" to my wife, the dogs would immediately run around looking for their leashes. I then modified the sentence to say, "let's go for a W – A – L – K." That lasted for several weeks. Then the dogs got it. I could do the same using different languages and it would take them very little time to figure out what I was talking about.

If you know about the psychology of learning, you could say to me, yes, but that is just associative learning, where the dog learns to associate a word with an object or action. That's just the same as telling a dog to sit and then giving the dog a reward of praise when the dog actually sits. No big deal. But then I can ask you: How do we learn languages? Don't we learn languages the same way? A young baby says her first word, "Mama," and the parents whoop and scream and yell, picking up the baby and giving her kisses and telling her what a smart baby she is. So the baby learns to say "Mama" to both parents. And the parents start teaching the baby to say "Mama" to the female parent by rewarding the baby whenever she says it in the appropriate context.

We don't know at this point how much of dog language is learned and how much of it is instinctive. Studies have shown that chihuahuas can understand the signals of St. Bernards, and vice versa. So there must be a strong instinctive component. But we have an instinctive component in our verbal language as well. Our brain can distinguish where one word ends and another word begins, even though that is very difficult to show on machines that analyze human speech. And much of human body language seems to be unlearned or instinctive.

Dogs talk to each other and to people in a variety of different ways. One way is through body language: body positions of the ears, tail, head, face, and general body posture. But wait, you say. You said the dogs have a language, and body language is not the same thing as a language. I beg to differ.

We humans talk to each other all the time, but in the process of talking we wave our arms around, we change our facial features, we adjust our posture, we smile, we frown, and we make eye contact with people. Some studies have shown that among people who know each other, spoken language conveys only 10 percent of the meaning

of a conversation and 90 percent of the meaning is conveyed through body language. Maybe this is why people have a harder time communicating through a visual platform like Zoom or through a nonvisual platform like email.

Another way that dogs communicate is through sound. Everybody knows that dogs bark, growl, and whine. But surprisingly enough these vocalizations haven't been studied very much. We know that high-pitched whines can be signs of anxiety or they can be signs of happiness and approval. We know that growls can be threatening, but they can also be used in the context of play. We know that barks can be signs of warning or aggression, but they also can be used in greeting, play, or expressions of pain.

Studies have shown that people are not very good at interpreting the vocalizations of dogs. Distinguishing a bark that uses an aggressive signal from a bark that is used as a play signal is hard for us. It's very easy for dogs.

A third way that dogs communicate with each other is through odors. Dogs have noses that are between 10,000 and 100,000 times more sensitive than our noses. Where we smell nothing at all, or per-

haps just a faint odor of something that we can't quite identify, dogs smell a huge landscape of odors: how many different species of animals passed by, how many different individual dogs were there, the age and gender of the dogs, their state of health, and a whole range of different environmental factors such as the different smells of the earth, the smell of the wind, and the smell of vegetation. Some researchers say that dogs can even sort out the scents of complex flavors into their simpler components.

This is why when we take our dogs out for a walk, the dogs want to stop and smell every fence post, every fire hydrant, and practically every tree and every bush. They are smelling the who, what, and when of everything that was there or everything that passed by. We read the news on our digital devices. Dogs read the news through the odors in their immediate environment.

When I would take my two poodles out for a walk, I would let them stop and sniff wherever they wanted. I knew how important it was for them. And I would look at other people who had their dogs on a leash and were hurrying them along, yanking them every time the dog wanted to sniff something, and I would always want to say: "Stop! Don't do that! Give your dog a break!" But to do that I would have to give people a long-winded explanation about how dogs like to smell things, and the bottom line usually was neither I nor they had the time for such explanations.

Because dogs live in an environment where odors are so important, it's hard for us to imagine what the world of odor is for a dog. We can't smell where other people have been, much less smell things like cancers, bombs, drugs, and even the poop of whales from half a mile away. Dogs can do all of that. They can also smell us and identify our typical body odor, as well as our general physiological condition. When I would be sick with something or other and lying either in bed or in my recliner chair, my dogs would mill around me, sometimes crawling into my lap, as if to say, here we are, we know that you don't feel well, and we're trying to make you better. I have no doubt that they pick up my feeling poorly through their great sense of smell. I just smell different when I'm sick.

While we can't strike up a conversation with dogs using odors, we can talk to them through two sensory modalities that are more relevant to us: vision, and sound. But we have to remember that dogs don't see things the same way that we do. We have three color receptors in our eyes: one for blue, one for yellow, and one for red. This is why we see the world in such dynamic colors.

Dogs have only two receptors: one for blue and one for green. They don't see red the way we do. To them, red is just a shade of gray or black. If we want to communicate with dogs through colors, we have to be very judicious as to what colors we choose. Red is out; green, blue, and yellow are in. And in case we get a swelled head of superiority over the vision of dogs, let me remind you that birds and many insects have four color receptors, one of which can see in the ultraviolet beyond what we can see, and octopuses have eight color receptors, giving them a colorful landscape that boggles my mind.

Dogs do better than we do with sound. The best of us humans can hear sound frequencies in the range of 20 Hertz (or cycles per second; Hertz is a unit of sound that describes the frequency or pitch of the sound) to 20,000 Hertz. Most of us are doing great if we can hear up to about 12,000 Hertz. Just for comparison, middle C on a piano

is 262 Hertz, and the highest A note on a piano is 3,520 Hertz. Dogs can hear up to between 45,000 and 65,000 Hertz, in what is called ultrasound. Most of our spoken words lie somewhere between 200 and 6,000 Hertz.

Maybe to a dog, our saying something like "Good boy!" sounds more like the rumble of a whale having gastric distress, or maybe the same thing that we hear when we hear the really low-pitched songs of humpback whales. I remember reading about ultrasonic whistles that people use to call their dogs. The idea is that the ultrasonic whistle is something that the dog hears but people can't hear and so it doesn't disturb anybody around the whistler, the way that a loud audible whistle would. The article pointed out that many people eventually throw away their ultrasonic whistles because they're not really sure whether the whistles work or not because they can't hear them.

But however dogs actually hear our words, they respond to them. So we have two ways that we can talk to dogs. We can talk to them with our words or the sounds that we make, we can adjust our meaning using different tones, and we can talk to them through visual signals such as waving our hands around, changing our facial expressions, or changing our posture.

2

HOW I GOT STARTED
WITH DOGS

I have always loved animals. When I was a small child, my father would bring home a variety of animals that he would find that were injured and needed help. Because my grandfather was a surgeon who also liked animals, he would patch up these animals and they would wander around the house briefly or sit in makeshift cages until they could be released again (there were no veterinarians near my home at that time). I remember meeting a variety of birds and some larger animals such as rabbits and foxes. My father would also bring home a varied selection of insects for me to look at. I still have a scar on my thumb from a huge (for a three-year-old child) Indonesian praying mantis that I unwisely grabbed and got my thumb slashed with the mantis's front legs.

My parents had a small black dog, a toy English spaniel, who was called "Little Fly" because she was marginally bigger than some of the flies that would occasionally invade our house. Little Fly hated children. At some point when I was too young to remember, one of the neighborhood children picked up Little Fly by her tail and injured her spine. Although her spine recovered after that experience, it cemented in her mind that little kids meant pain and trouble.

I loved Little Fly. My first practical exposure to applied dog behavior (as a three- and four-year-old) was to try to figure out a way to make Little Fly love me. This required a lot of patience and learning that when she would growl at me, I had to back off and let her see that I meant no harm. Gradually, by approaching her slowly, offering her treats, and not pushing the issue until she was ready to trust me, I got

her to like jumping into my lap and being stroked. She still hated kids in general, but I was an exception in her mind.

Little Fly died of old age when I was ten, and I went through a dogless period where I mostly played with my parents' friends' dogs. I seemed to have an intuitive feeling for what was bothering the dogs, and I always made suggestions to my parents' friends about what they could do to improve their dogs' lives. This was a time when people thought that training dogs had to be done with some brutality, and most of the time my suggestions of treating the dogs kindly, with love, affection, and treats, fell on deaf ears. Occasionally someone would try my suggestions and then would marvel to friends what a changed animal their dog had become.

My formal exposure to the world of training dogs occurred when I was in my twenties, when I was a student living in Berkeley and studying at the University of California, where one of my fields of study was animal behavior. My parents lived in San Francisco and, missing me, encouraged me to drop by frequently.

To lessen their separation anxiety, I got them a miniature poodle puppy. My mother immediately immersed herself in training the puppy, taking classes in dog training, having training sessions with friends, and showing the dog at dog shows. When I visited my parents, which was fairly often, I would go along to the training sessions and the shows to watch what was happening. I was particularly impressed that many of the people that I watched seemed to love their dogs, but they also treated them without a shred of kindness, yelling at them, jerking their leashes, and often treating them as objects rather than as sentient beings. The priority at dog shows often seemed to be that the dogs should win a ribbon rather than that the dogs were happy.

This experience caused me to study all of the dog behavior and dog training books that I could get my hands on. I was already well versed in animal behavior and learning theory from my undergraduate and graduate studies, and I tried to find out how people were applying learning theory on a practical basis.

I could see the parallels between the animal behavior that I learned in my coursework and the practical manifestation of that in the behavior of the dogs that I was observing. However, I was amazed at the variety of advice that was provided in the dog training books, and how some of the advice was completely contrary to what people were finding with the behavior of other animals.

The more I studied the dog books and the literature on dog behavior, behavior problems, and behavior solutions, the more I realized that opinions varied all over the map and that the situation must have been horribly confusing to people who wanted to do the right thing but didn't know where to go to find good information.

Even as a child I had been interested in communication. I found that I could always intuitively understand the body language of animals. Later, when I was studying animal behavior, I found that there were solid principles behind my understanding.

Later, as a university faculty member and researcher exploring animal behavior, I applied this understanding to consulting with people about their companion animals. I found that reading the body language of their pets helped me to assess what might be the problem. Often I realized that the people I talked to had a completely different perception of the problem than what I was able to assess. Once they understood the real problem, I helped them take the appropriate measures to ensure that they and their animals could begin living in harmony.

Along the way, I realized that many of the behavioral problems that I was seeing were the result of incorrect training methods. So I started offering dog training classes based on the concepts of positive reinforcement, no punishment, and information about dog behavior. Because I

thought that it was important for dogs to socialize, I always had several minutes of dog mixers, both before and after class, where the dogs and the people could socialize. This created a friendly environment among both the dogs and the people, and everyone had a great time. Dogs and people always looked forward to class.

Now I am often asked by people how they can get into the field of applied dog behavior. My answer is for them to learn as much as they can about animal behavior, dog behavior, dog communication, and learning theory, and then work with dogs in practical settings where they can get experience solving problems. All dogs have a set of behaviors that are unique to dogs and another set of behaviors that are found in common with other animal species, which is why it is important to study both animal behavior and dog behavior.

However, within that set of behaviors, every dog is different according to his or her personality, and every dog has his or her own challenges, often linked to the particular situation in which they live. I believe that the more experience and knowledge people have, the more they will realize that a cookie-cutter, one-size-fits-all formula doesn't work across the board for all dogs and that practical solutions have to be tailored to the personality of each dog and the circumstances of their home and family environment.

Above all, however, I feel that an important feature is that people who get into this field should like dogs, respect them as individual beings, and like the animals that they work with. Love and rewards go a much longer way than hate, distrust, and punishment.

3

HOW TO READ YOUR DOG

B ody movements are a very important component of dog language. Dogs can move their tail, their body stance, and their facial features such as their eyes, ears, and mouth to signal a variety of moods and intentions. Just like we have words that we string into sentences, dogs have body movements that they combine into meaningful communication.

In human body language, all of the movements of the body come together into something that conveys information. Looking at just one signal, such as the eyes, is not very meaningful by itself without considering what the other body parts are doing. It's the same with isolated words. If I told you just the word "fire," you would not grasp what I was trying to say. Was I trying to tell you that your house was on fire? That you should fire someone? That I just fired a gun? Without additional words, you wouldn't know what I was trying to say. So it is with dogs. Each movement has to be considered together with all the other movements to get the meaning of a dog sentence.

However, before we can put words into sentences, we have to learn how to spell those words and what each word, taken by itself, can possibly mean.

This is why I am breaking down the signals that dogs send in their body language into their component parts, so that you can look at each signal and get a general sense of what it could mean. Once you have learned the possible meanings of each of the signals, you can begin to combine all of the signals into meaningful dog sentences. You can finally begin to understand what your dog is trying to say to you!

11

THE TAIL

Everybody knows that dogs wag their tail. What many people don't necessarily know is that how dogs wag their tails is important, both for communicating information to other dogs and to people.

One common way that people get bitten is when they see a dog wagging her tail, think the dog is friendly, and approach her, sometimes even hugging her. But all wags are not friendly. If the dog has her tail partially raised and is wagging the tail slowly back and forth, that may very well be a sign of potential aggression. Under those circumstances, it's important to look at what else is happening with the dog's body language to get an overall picture of whether the dog intends to bite or perhaps the dog is just lazy about wagging her tail on a hot summer day.

How good are people at interpreting the behavior of dogs? Dogs and people have been around together for perhaps fifty thousand years, so you would think that people would be pretty good at it.

One study tested sixty people in the vicinity of Edinburgh, Scotland, on their ability to interpret dog behavior.

The sixty people were divided into four groups: dog owners, veterinarians, dog trainers, and non-dog-owners. The non-dog-owners had no experience with dogs, while the others had considerable experience. Dog owners had a median of thirty years of experience, dog trainers had a median of twenty years of experience, and veterinarians had a median of eleven years of experience.

The authors of the study first walked a border collie past eight other dogs on separate occasions and recorded video clips of the responses of the other dogs to the border collie. They then categorized the responses of the dogs as aggressive, confident, fearful, friendly, submissive, play solicitation, actual play, defensive, or indifferent.

The sixty people were shown the video clips and asked to describe the behaviors. As we can predict from the long association between dogs and humans, both dog-oriented people and non-dog people had similar descriptions of what the dogs' behaviors meant. Except for two categories of behavior (confidence and play solicitation), there were no significant differences in the descriptions of any of the behaviors.

The amazing thing is that both the dog-oriented people and the non-dog people got many of the behaviors wrong.

Both the dog-oriented people and the non-dog people could mostly identify indifferent (90 percent of observers scored correctly) and friendly behavior (73 percent scored correctly). Fearful behavior was correctly identified by 67 percent of the observers, and play solicitation behavior was correctly identified by 62 percent.

However, for the other behaviors, both the dog-oriented people and the non-dog people got things mostly wrong. Aggression was correctly identified by only 38 percent of the observers, confident behavior was also identified by only 38 percent, and actual play (as opposed to play solicitation) was correctly identified by only 30 percent of the observers.

Most of the observers seemed to focus primarily on the movement of the tail rather than on all of the other signals that a dog was displaying.

Both to people and to dogs, the tail represents an important signal of a dog's mood, state of mind, and intentions.

Docking or cutting off a part of the tail interferes with this signal. A docked tail is often just a stump that is really hard to see. My two standard poodles had their tails docked before I got them. Otherwise I would never have permitted that to happen. Their tails were about three inches long, and when the dogs were groomed, the groomer routinely left a big tuft of hair at the end of the tail so that what the tail was doing was much more visible. The groomer explained that this was part of the beauty of the cut. I had a different explanation. The tuft allowed me to see what the tail was doing. In some breeds, however, it is either too short for a tuft or it isn't acceptable practice, and so the tail is an almost invisible stump.

This not only makes it hard for people to see what the tail is doing, it also makes it hard for dogs to see.

What happens when the tail is artificially shortened or docked? How much are other dogs affected by this tail shortening? In the United States at least, more than one-third of all dog breeds have traditionally had their tails docked. What does this do to dog body language?

This has been a difficult question to answer scientifically because experiments have been so hard to perform. If you're using live dogs with short and long tails to study this question, you have a lot of factors other than tail length that could confuse the issue. You have all kinds of body scents, ear positions, general body posture, and behavioral interactions that can modify the response of other dogs to short or long tails.

A recent behavioral tool has been to use animal-like robots to study the behavior of other animals. With a robot, you can test for specific things, such as a short tail versus a long tail on a robot that looks like a dog, and everything else stays constant—the robot is still the same size, stays in the same position, doesn't have any confusing smells, and doesn't engage in any behaviors that could modify the response of an approaching animal.

Using a robot, a study has looked at the effect of short and long tails on the approach behavior of other dogs. The experimenters did this study in a place where there are a lot of off-leash dogs in Victoria, British Columbia, Canada. They used a robot about the size of a Labrador

retriever and attached to the robot either a short tail (9 centimeters or 3.5 inches) or a long tail (30 centimeters or 12 inches). Using a servo mechanism, they could make the tail either wag or stand still. They videotaped the approaches of off-leash dogs and assessed the conditions under which the dogs either freely approached the robot or hesitated in their approach.

They divided the approaching dogs into two categories: smaller dogs whose shoulder was below the shoulder of the robot and larger dogs whose shoulder was above that of the robot.

They found that the dogs differed in their approach to a short tail versus a long tail.

Both larger and smaller dogs tended to approach the robot without hesitation when the robot had a long, wagging tail and tended to hesitate more when the long tail was motionless. We might expect this because a wagging tail generally signals friendliness, while a motionless tail can signal potential aggression.

On the other hand, both larger and smaller dogs seemed to have a difficult time determining whether the short tail was wagging or still. Both the larger and smaller dogs tended to approach either the wagging short tail or the still short tail at about the same rate, a rate that was below the rate of approach for a long wagging tail and above the rate of approach for a motionless long tail.

It was as if the dogs couldn't see the difference between a wagging short tail or a motionless one and had to make a guess as to whether to approach or not.

It seems that tail docking does introduce some confusion into dog language, making it much more difficult for dogs to determine whether a dog with a short tail is friendly or potentially aggressive.

Dogs that wag their tail more quickly can convey information as well. If you look at the arc of a dog's wagging tail and pay very close attention, you can see that the tail wags slightly more to either the right side of the dog or the left side. If the tail wags more to the left side of the dog, this is a signal that the dog is feeling uncertain or anxious. If the tail wags more to the right side, this is a signal that the dog is happy. Dogs can tell the difference. We humans usually need some practice in order to be able to see that, but once we do, we can get some good information about the psychological state of our dog.

The position of the tail is also important.

I got my standard poodle Zephyr when he was a twelve-week-old puppy. From the time that he entered our household, he got nothing but love and praise. This made him a very confident dog who was not afraid of anyone or anything. His tail always pointed straight up. And it was always wagging, usually to the right more than to the left.

My other standard poodle Raja was a rescue dog. He was abused as a puppy and then lived in a household with six other dogs, all of whom snarled, snapped, and bit him. When we first got him groomed his body was covered with painful mats of fur and he had scars from multiple dog bites. Not surprisingly, when he first came to us his tail was pressed straight down between his legs. As we lavished him with love and praise, gradually his tail started to come up to a horizontal position, considered to be a neutral position where the dog is neither scared nor happy. This took months. Eventually, his tail started to go into an upright position more and more, but he still did not wag his tail very enthusiastically.

This changed when my wife discovered Raja's passion in life. Before we adopted him, he had never played with a ball. And even though at our house we threw a ball for Zephyr, Raja never participated in this game. He simply didn't know what to do and would go and lie down somewhere while Zephyr was running around with the ball.

My wife thought, what if she could teach Raja to play catch with the ball? So while I took Zephyr out for walks, my wife would patiently show Raja the ball and throw it toward him over very short distances. At first, he didn't know what to do. The ball just bounced off his muzzle. But then one time he opened his mouth while the ball was coming toward it and he caught the ball. Hallelujah! He suddenly caught on and from that point on it became the most important game in his life.

Perhaps because he had much more practice at it, Zephyr was much better at catching a ball than Raja. But he apparently realized how important the game was to Raja, and when we would throw a ball to the two of them, Zephyr always let Raja either catch the ball first or run after the ball and retrieve it first. And when Raja was catching or chasing a ball, his tail always wagged enthusiastically much more to the right.

HOW TO READ YOUR DOG

TAIL

- What is the position of the tail? Is it held up pointed at the sky (confidence), is it held horizontal to the position of the dog (neutral, the dog is neither confident nor scared), or is it held down toward the ground, in extreme cases held between the dog's legs (fear)?

- How fast is the tail wagging? Is it wagging slowly back and forth in a slightly upright condition (potentially aggressive) or is it wagging fast (either happy or anxious)?

- Is the tail wagging more to the right (happy) or to the left (anxious)?

THE HEAD

Let's continue our survey of dogs' visual signals with a discussion of the head and body posture.

A dog can hold her head in several different positions that are indicative of what the dog is experiencing. If the head is raised up, the dog is feeling either confident, aggressive, or happy. As the head moves downward, this shows that the dog is increasingly less confident, less aggressive, or less happy. Ultimately, if the head is down so that the nose is practically touching the ground, it indicates that the dog is very unhappy or very scared.

Moving the head to one side can indicate that the dog is not very confident. This usually occurs in the context of when someone is looking directly at the dog, and instead of looking directly at the person or another dog, the dog moves her head to one side to avoid a direct stare. Sometimes a dog will repeatedly move her head from one side to another to avoid looking directly at the object that is making her feel uncomfortable.

Another head movement is the head tilt. This happens when the dog is listening intently and paying attention to someone. The head gets tilted to either the right side or the left side, and the dog looks directly at whoever is in front of her. This is a signal that says, I am paying attention to you, I am listening to what you have to say, but I'm not a threat to you. Curiously enough, we see the head tilt in people as well when they are paying attention to someone but want to indicate that they are not threatening.

Whenever I talked to my standard poodle Raja, he would always tilt his head to his left side and look intently at me. On the other hand, my standard poodle Zephyr would never tilt his head when I was talking to him.

This might have been a reflection of their different histories. As I mentioned previously, my wife and I got Zephyr when he was twelve weeks old, as a puppy, and then my wife spent much of the next year raising Zephyr, working on teaching him various commands and generally treating him well so that he grew up as a confident dog. He felt that he was an equal member of the family, expecting to be treated with consideration. He loved to watch my wife cook and was always in the kitchen as she was preparing meals. We laughingly called him "Zef the Chef" because he was so interested in the cooking process. He also loved going for rides in the car and trying to stand with his front feet balanced on the console between the seats, looking out at traffic. I often had the impression that he thought that he could do a better job of driving a car than I could.

Raja on the other hand was a rescue dog, who was a year and a half old when we got him from a lady who was about to euthanize him. She ran her own informal dog rescue business from her home, where he was part of a pack of six dogs who ran free through their rural neighborhood and generally terrorized anyone in the immediate vicinity. Raja was a latecomer to the group, which made him the "odd man out." To show their displeasure with him, the other dogs regularly harassed and bit him and kept him away from the food that the lady provided. Because he didn't fit in with the rest of the dog pack, the lady was going to euthanize him; but when we found out, we convinced her to turn him over to us.

It took a long time for us to build up Raja's confidence. At first, he was terrified of Zephyr. We spent weeks working on getting them acquainted, and gradually he started to trust us and trust that Zephyr would not attack him. But he never had the same confidence level as Zephyr. That is probably why he would always turn his head to one side when I was talking to him.

HOW TO READ YOUR DOG

HEAD

- Head is up: The dog is confident, happy, or aggressive.
- Head is down: The dog is scared, depressed, or anxious.

GENERAL BODY POSTURE

Like the head, the body posture can assume several positions.

If the dog's body is raised up, into a completely upright position, and the dog's legs are extended straight up into almost a stilt-like position, this indicates that the dog is feeling aggressive. Usually when this happens, the fur on the back of the neck and on most of the back of the dog is raised up. We say then that the dog has his hackles raised.

On the other hand, if the dog's body is in an upright position but the legs are not stiff and the hackles aren't raised, the dog is feeling confident and relaxed.

As with the head, as the dog increasingly feels fear or a lack of confidence, the body gets lowered more and more toward the ground. Extreme fear will lead the dog to lie down completely on the ground. This fear is also signaled by facial features, such as the ears being flattened and pulled back into a backward position, the pupils of the eyes being dilated, and the mouth commissure—the corners of the mouth—pulled back. In human body language there is a parallel situation where people bow their heads or bow their torsos as a sign of respect and ultimately fear of another person. In extreme situations people will prostrate themselves flat on the ground as a sign of respect or fear.

Dogs exhibit this behavior of lying down with the ears flattened when they have gotten into something like the garbage and their person comes in and yells at them. Opinions differ about this. Some people say that the dog is responding to the person's tone of voice, remembering that that tone of voice previously led to punishment but not knowing why the person is yelling at him. According to this line of thought, dogs do not remember that they have done something like getting into the garbage, and consequently do not feel guilty about having done so. Other people suggest that dogs know perfectly well why they are being yelled at and do indeed feel guilty at the time, even if the guilt is something like, Oh no, I've been caught.

In my opinion, dogs will sometimes do things that will get them yelled at, just for the sake of attention or for the sake of expressing displeasure at something. My mother had a miniature poodle who went everywhere with her most of the time. However, there were times when my mother had to leave her dog home alone while she went to do errands where a dog would be inappropriate, such as a doctor's visit or going out with friends to a restaurant. Invariably, when my mother would return home, she would find that the poodle had taken all of the pillows off the couch and chairs and strewn them all over the floor. Fortunately, nothing was ever shredded. My mother always yelled at her dog when she found the pillows on the floor, and her dog always did the crouching behavior, but that never changed the dog's behavior whenever she was left alone.

Some people might say that this is simply separation anxiety, where the dog is worried about being left alone and takes her anxiety out on moving around the pillows. I think that the dog was making a deliberate statement: "You left me alone, and I resent it, so I'm going to move around all of the pillows, just to show you that I resent it."

One day, Raja got into the garbage while I was gone. The garbage can had a tight lid on it, opened by a foot treadle, and to make sure that the can was dog proof, I put a plastic gallon jug filled with water on top of the lid whenever no one was in the house. Raja knocked over the garbage can, sending the water jug flying, and somehow pried open the lid to get at the contents of the can. Fortunately, there was nothing in

there but wet paper towels, so he couldn't hurt himself by eating decaying garbage. He did have a great time shredding the paper towels and scattering the shreds over the living room rug.

On past occasions when this happened, I reprimanded Raja by scolding him in a deep, low voice, pointing to the shreds of garbage and telling him "No!" several times. I do not believe in hitting dogs, so the only punishment that Raja received was my stern and deep-voiced "No." Throughout his life, Raja had gotten into the garbage perhaps once or twice a year, so this was a relatively unusual event, triggered perhaps by absolute boredom.

When I walked into the house, Raja greeted me with his usual enthusiastic tail wagging at the door. I petted him, as is our usual custom, and then stepped into the living room, where I saw the shreds of paper.

I simply pointed to the garbage and looked at Raja. He immediately started to cringe, crouching down low, with his tail between his legs. I did not say a word but kept pointing to the papers scattered around. Raja then lay down on the floor and rolled over, exposing his belly, with his front feet folded up and his eyes closed.

When I have been asked about the proper thing to do with a dog who has gotten into the garbage hours or minutes before the dog's people come home, I have previously always said that the best thing is to do nothing, because by then the dog does not remember having strewn things around, and punishing the dog after the fact would be counterproductive. I have always said that the dog does not at that point understand what the punishment is about and would only get confused if punished. This is straight out of classical learning theory, where a response has to follow an event immediately for the lesson to be learned.

However, here was Raja clearly acting as if he knew that he had done something wrong. Not only that, but he was apparently remembering our last lesson about garbage from at least half a year before.

Does that mean that he knew right from wrong? And in the larger picture, do dogs in general know right from wrong? In *Wild Justice: The Moral Lives of Animals*, Marc Bekoff and his coauthor Jessica Pierce argue that dogs and other animals have a sense of right and wrong and a moral sense of fairness and empathy. Although the main thrust of the book deals with animals in general, Bekoff and Pierce have some examples from the behavior of dogs. They mention a case of a larger, stronger

male dog playing with a smaller, weaker male and restraining his bites so as to not injure the smaller dog. They also mention the work of Friedericke Range and her colleagues in Austria, who have shown that dogs will refuse to work for food if they see that other dogs are getting more for doing the same thing. Bekoff and Pierce give a number of other examples, ranging from elephants to mice, that show that animals have a sense of morality, compassion, and a sense of right or wrong.

So how about Raja and the garbage? Did he have a sense of right and wrong? I would say yes. I think that he knew perfectly well that he was not allowed to get into the garbage and perhaps felt a sense of remorse or shame when he was called on this issue. What's more, he remembered prior scoldings, even though they happened a long time ago, and knew that they applied to the current situation.

Just like I still remember being scolded as a kid for getting into things that my parents told me not to touch.

Another postural behavior that dogs do is they will lie down and expose their belly. The dog is essentially saying, here is my most vulnerable part of my body, and I trust you not to hurt me. As a general rule, dogs who have more aggressive predispositions will be reluctant to lie down and expose their belly. Dogs who are more gentle and submissive are much more willing to do this kind of behavior. While the evidence for what the dog gets out of this behavior is sparse, observationally it looks like the dog usually enjoys having his belly rubbed by someone he trusts.

As with head turning, Raja and Zephyr were different about having their belly rubbed. Raja would frequently turn over on his back and let us rub his belly. Zephyr was just the opposite. He never turned over. I could rub his belly when he was lying down, but I had to do it by inserting my hand between the floor and the dog. I did it rarely, because

I had the sense that he didn't particularly like having his belly rubbed. Once again, it came down to a question of confidence.

One postural behavior that dogs will adopt when they feel uncomfortable in a situation is sitting down. This is part of a set of signals that have been characterized as calming signals, first proposed by Turid Rugaas. She said that dogs have a variety of signals that are designed to defuse an aggressive or uncomfortable situation.

Sitting is one of those signals. When a dog encounters another dog who is aggressive, or a person who is yelling or otherwise intimidating the dog, she will sit down. This is in effect saying, I'm not a threat, I'm not going to respond aggressively, and why don't you just settle down. Sitting also cuts off access by other dogs to the dog's anal glands, which might be pumping out chemical signals of fear or of any other physiological response that might provoke an aggressive dog.

I frequently go on morning walks at a nearby state park where people walk their dogs. This gives me an opportunity to see how dogs and their people respond when meeting another dog and their person. The state park mandates that all dogs have to be on leashes—dogs can't just run up to another dog, they have to follow the constraints of their leashes. Sometimes I see a person with a confident, enthusiastic dog come up to talk to someone who has a shy dog. The shy dog can't go anywhere because of the leash. He has to interact with the other dog. While the confident dog is trying to sniff the shy dog's anus, the shy dog will often sit down. That behavior will instantly calm down the confident dog, who then either stands near the shy one and doesn't do anything or finds something else to interest him.

There are a number of other calming signals.

Licking the lips is one that can also be seen in human body language when people are frightened, uncomfortable, or uncertain about the situation that they are in.

Another important signal is yawning. Dogs don't yawn because they are bored. They yawn because they are stressed. This might also be a part of human body language, although the evidence for that for people is somewhat less clear.

A third calming signal is lifting up a paw. We see this as something that is very cute, and most people think that the dog is trying to shake hands with them. The reality is that the dog is feeling somewhat uncomfortable and wants to defuse the situation by offering a paw.

A fourth calming signal is looking away. Even if the dog doesn't turn her head to one side or the other, she might look away so as to not look directly at whatever is making her feel uncomfortable. We see this signal and often think that the dog isn't paying attention. Commonly in that circumstance people will yell at the dog and reprimand the dog for her lack of attention, not realizing that that only increases the dog's insecurity about the situation.

A fifth calming signal is a shake-off, where the dog will shake vigorously as if his fur is wet and he is trying to dry himself. This is probably done as a way of releasing muscle tension that builds up during an uncomfortable situation. While in human body language you don't see people going around shaking themselves vigorously every time they have an uncomfortable situation with their boss, teacher, or spouse, shaking as a way of loosening muscle tension is sometimes taught as a prelude to relaxation.

A sixth calming signal is scratching. A dog might be interacting vigorously with another dog and then suddenly stop and scratch at his neck or shoulder. This is another way of relieving built-up tension. In animal behavior terms, this behavior is known as displacement behavior, which is exhibiting a behavior that is inappropriate to a particular situation. One author who has written about dog behavior has described watching two dogs running on opposite sides of the fence, snarling and barking their heads off as if they wanted to kill each other. Then one dog stopped, sat down, and scratched his neck. The other dog politely waited until the scratching was finished, not barking or snarling. When the scratching ended, both dogs went back to running along the fence barking and snarling as if they wanted to tear each other into bits.

We have similar kinds of calming signals. We look away from someone when emotions become intense. We sit down to create a calmer situation so that we are not towering over someone. We lick our lips and play with our hair when we feel uncertain or not confident in a particular situation. We yawn when we are bored, but yawning is contagious—when one person yawns other people tend to yawn, so yawning may be a group calming signal.

HOW TO READ YOUR DOG

BODY POSTURE

- Body raised, legs straight like stilts: The dog is aggressive.
- Body raised, legs normal, relaxed: The dog is confident, happy.
- Body lowered: The dog is afraid.
- Body on ground, belly on ground: The dog is extremely afraid.
- Body on ground, belly up: The dog is feeling submissive, wants reassuring pats.

DOG PLAY

When dogs play, they run around chasing each other, biting, snarling, and barking. A lot of times it looks like an aggressive encounter between two or more dogs. In fact, studies have shown that people are remarkably bad at telling the difference between when dogs are playing and when dogs are actually fighting. But dogs can tell the difference.

One important signal that play is about to begin is the play bow. A dog who wants to play will lower her head and shoulders, stretching out the body with the rump and tail high in the air. This is a mixed message signal. Lowering the head in the front part of the body says, I'm afraid and I'm not confident, while at the same time having the rump and tail raised says I'm very confident. The message it sends to other dogs is that no matter what I do, I'm not going to hurt you and we're going to have a good time playing.

But the play bow is not the only signal that dogs give to solicit play. One study videotaped the interactions of dogs playing in a dog park where all the dogs were off leash to see what kinds of signals dogs send to each other when they want to play.

The study found that playing dogs used several different signals to indicate to each other that they were playing. These included a play bow, an open-mouth play face, a head bow, a play slap with the forelegs slapping the ground, and a leap-on or jumping up and putting the front paws around the other dog's head.

But sometimes one of the dogs appeared to lose interest. Then the other dog used attention-getting signals to restart the play behavior. These signals included placing the body near the other dog's face, making a backward leap, turning around so that the dog's rear end was next to the other dog's face, bumping into the dog, touching the other dog with nose and closed mouth, biting the other dog with a soft bite, making biting movements in the air, pawing at the other dog, and barking.

Sometimes the dog who stopped playing was not looking at the dog who wanted to continue to play. When that happened, the dog who wanted the play to continue did not use visual attention-getting signals such as placing the body near the dog's face or making a backward leap. Instead the dog used tactile signals such as bumping, touching the nose to the other dog's body, or biting with a soft bite.

The results of this study show that dogs understand that when another dog is not looking at them, it is better to use touch as a communication tool rather than using visual signals.

While we humans don't have the equivalent of a play bow to indicate that we want to play, children have a number of signals, both

vocal and tactile, that they give to each other when they're playing. They push each other, yell at each other, and chase each other. In some cases, children will wrestle with each other in what looks like fights. Perhaps just like people assessing play behavior with dogs and getting it wrong, thinking that it's aggressive behavior, maybe somebody who's not familiar with human behavior can get play behavior wrong as well.

HOW TO READ YOUR DOG

DOG PLAY

- Front part of the body is down toward the ground, hind end up: The dog wants to play.
- The dog makes quick circles around itself: The dog wants to play.
- The dog bumps into another dog briefly, then runs away: The dog wants to play.

DOG FACES

Dogs have very expressive faces. And just like with us, different parts of a dog's face signal information to both other dogs and us. Just as with us, it is best to look at what is happening with the dog's entire face rather than concentrating only on specific features.

For example, in human body language when a person smiles, the corners of the mouth go up, the eyes crinkle and partially shut, and the face becomes slightly rounder. Looking at only one of these cues, such as the smiling mouth, is a mistake. People can fake a smile with their mouth, but if the other features on the face don't correspondingly move, other people can subconsciously recognize that the smile is faked. While we don't know whether dogs can fake their expressions, it is safer to look at the whole face in judging what the dog is trying to communicate.

The relevant parts that are involved in this signaling are the ears, the eyes, and the mouth. Let's take a look at each one of these.

THE EARS

If you watch a dog for a little bit, you'll see that his ears are constantly moving. Some breeds have what are called prick ears, where the ears are erect and stand up straight above the head. Other breeds have floppy ears, where the ears hang down from the side of the head. Prick ears are typical of wolves who were once the ancestors of dogs, while floppy ears are a product of the domestication of the dog.

Both types of ears move, but the movement of the floppy ears is much harder to see.

All puppies are born with floppy ears. At about six to ten weeks the cartilage in the ears of a number of breeds starts to strengthen and the ears start to become upright. In other breeds, such as poodles and spaniels, the ears never become upright and remain floppy.

Some breeds are born with floppy ears but then the ears are surgically manipulated in a process called cropping so that they stand up straight. This is commonly done to breeds such as the Doberman pinscher, boxers, Great Danes, and some terriers. The rationale for this is that these dogs were used for agricultural purposes or for dogfights, and floppy ears could get caught in vegetation or be bitten by an opponent dog. Because dogfights are illegal and it is unlikely that dog ears would get caught up in vegetation, the main reason for cropping the ears is that it conforms to the breed standards of what that dog should look like.

However, there is another reason. Whether the people who work with these dogs realize it or not, they get a lot of cues from the ears. And floppy ears don't provide as many cues as erect ears.

I had this demonstrated to me very clearly one time when some friends brought over their greyhound. We met them in our garden, along with some other friends and our two standard poodles. I got a little bit bored with the conversation and started paying attention to what the ears of the dogs were doing. The greyhound's ears were constantly moving back and forth and to each side, both in response to noises in the ambient environment and to voices occasionally raised in excitement as one person or another was making a point.

I could see the greyhound's ears moving very clearly. On the other hand, my two poodles, who were standing right next to the greyhound, looked like their ears weren't moving at all. It was only after I focused on their ears that I noticed that there were slight movements, up and down and sideways, paralleling the more obvious movements of the greyhound's ears. I had to look really hard to see the movements of the poodles' ears, and I'm pretty sure that the greyhound had an equally hard time seeing what the poodles' ears were doing.

Because dog ears are capable of very subtle movements, my guess is that those subtle movements convey a lot of meaningful information

to other dogs. However, such subtle movement of the ears has not been studied. We are left with interpreting only the large-scale movements of the ears.

Here is what we know about dog ears. If the ears are upright and pointing forward, this means that the dog is interested, paying attention, or feeling aggressive. If the ears are upright but pointed to the side, the dog is relaxed and generally listening in on all of the ambient sounds going on around her. If the ears are flattened and pointed back, the dog is either anxious or scared. Unfortunately, dogs with floppy ears are much harder to read in this respect.

Dog ears can produce what animal behaviorists call a graded signal. This is a signal that is not either on or off but has a number of different intermediate conditions that provide subtle information. In the gross sense, ears upright and pointing forward is a large contrast between ears flattened and pointing back, but the reality is that the dog has a large number of positions between those two endpoints, and those many positions can signal subtle changes in the dog's mood or attention. The best way to identify all of these different positions is to study your dog carefully while your dog is responding to different things: your praise, the presence of food, a strange person or a strange dog, and different noises in your house or outside. This will give you information about the subtle positions that your dog's ears can take in different contexts.

HOW TO READ YOUR DOG

PRICK EARS

- Ears up and facing forward: The dog is either paying specific attention to something or feeling aggressive.
- Ears up and pointed to the side: The dog is relaxed and paying general attention to what is happening around her.
- Ears back and flat: The dog is scared.

HOW TO READ YOUR DOG

FLOPPY EARS

- The same principles apply, but difficult to see the ear movements.

THE EYES

Unlike people, most dogs have very little white in their eyes. The white in human eyes can indicate where a person is looking because white as a color is something that people spot immediately at a distance. With dogs, it's not so easy to see what they are looking at from far away.

Close up, however, it's a lot easier to see what a dog is looking at. At the center of the eye is a black pupil, which is surrounded by a brown, blue, or yellow iris, and then outside of that is the white of the eye known as the sclera.

Under most circumstances, the white is not very visible. It becomes more visible when the dog is feeling scared, uncomfortable, or threatened. This is known in dog body language as the "whale eye." The eyelids become rounder and the dog moves his head slightly to the side while looking at something that has made him feel uncomfortable. This side movement exposes the sclera and makes the white much more visible.

Most dogs do not like to be stared at by people they don't know. A direct stare from a person or another dog is taken as an aggressive challenge. A stare can either frighten a more timid dog or cause a more assertive dog to act aggressively. Upon encountering a strange dog, the best strategy is to look to the side and view the dog out of the corner of your eye. Avoid looking directly at the dog's face. Otherwise, there is a real danger of being bitten. Once a dog knows you and builds a relationship with you, the dog is usually okay with you looking directly into his eyes.

When I was a college student, I discovered that people do not like being stared at, just like dogs. I was taking an introductory philosophy class. Previously, I had read a lot of philosophy and liked the subject, so I eagerly sat in the front row and raptly watched the professor as he was talking at the lectern. I knew the material that he was presenting, so I did not feel the need to take notes. I just sat and watched, admiring how he was taking difficult concepts and simplifying them so that the class could understand.

After several lectures, the professor glanced occasionally in my direction. I thought nothing of it. Then he started looking at me for longer periods of time. Not knowing what to do, I simply looked back. Finally, he stopped his lecture, came up to my chair, crouched down in front of me, used his hands to pry open both of his eyes as much as they would open, and said, "How would you like to be stared at all the time?" I couldn't think of an answer, so I just stared back. He huffed and said, "Don't do it again!" after which he returned to the lectern to continue his lecture. I was stunned.

For the rest of the course, I sat in the back of the room by the windows. It was spring, and birds were nesting in the trees outside. I found that watching the birds was much more entertaining. It turned out to be an enjoyable class, and I never looked at the professor again.

Opening the eye so that it is rounder and doesn't blink produces what is known as a "hard eye" or almost a fixed stare. This is a sign that the dog is feeling either threatened or aggressive and can bite if provoked.

If the dog is scared, the pupil area enlarges so that the dog looks like he has large black eyes. This is very similar to what happens when people get scared: their eyes open wide and their pupils dilate, leading to the expression "eyes wide with fear."

When the dog is feeling relaxed, the eyes are said to be "soft," which means that the eyelids are less round and the pupils are not dilated.

One of the facial features that is associated with the eyes is the so-called puppy dog eyes, where the dog's eyebrows go up. To us, this

makes the dog look much more appealing and we think that the dog is pleading for something, such as perhaps a treat or a walk or some attention. This resonates with us because our eyebrows go up when we are asking for something or expressing surprise.

My standard poodle Raja always had this expression when he was asking me to throw his ball. He would come up to me with his ball in his mouth, look me directly in the face, and raise eyebrows, as if saying, "Won't you please throw my ball for me, please, please, please?" Even though I was usually busy, the expression on his face would usually make me relent and throw the ball. It was just too cute. I just couldn't say no.

Unfortunately, a new study has shown that dogs raising their eyebrows are not actually asking for anything, or pleading, or trying to be cute. It turns out that raising the eyebrows is just a part of the musculature of the face that gets triggered when the dog is looking *upward*. Even after I found that out, I still thought that it was cute.

Because dogs have lived with humans for such a long time, they apparently adapted to paying attention to where people look and also looking in that direction. Because the whites of our eyes send such a clear signal about where we are looking, it's relatively easy for dogs to notice our eye movements and look in the same direction. Even though dogs evolved from wolves, wolves can't notice our eyes the way that dogs can. Studies have shown that when we move our eyes in particular directions, wolves pay no attention.

HOW TO READ YOUR DOG

EYES

- Eyes round, staring, white of eye very visible: The dog is uncomfortable or feeling aggressive.
- Eye pupils expanded into large black circles: The dog is frightened.
- Eyes slightly squinted, pupils normal sized: The dog is relaxed.

THE MOUTH

A dog's mouth is a source of many signals. Like the ears, the signals are graded ones, which means that the signals aren't either on or off but have a number of subtle stages in between.

Technically the lips at the corners of a dog's mouth are known as the mouth commissure. The mouth could be entirely open or entirely closed or have different stages between being open and closed. As with the other facial signals, it's important to notice what is going on with the entire face and not rely entirely on what is going on with the mouth.

If the mouth is mostly closed but the lips are pulled back in the front half of the lips, exposing the canine teeth, the dog is being aggressive and is likely to bite. On the other hand, if the dog's mouth is slightly open and the lips and commissures are pulled back along the entire length of the mouth, the dog is expressing fear and is also likely to bite, out of fear and not out of aggression.

The mouth can be open, with the tongue extended either slightly or a lot. That indicates that the dog is confident and relaxed.

Dogs can also laugh.

Sometimes I like to think about the question, do dogs have a sense of humor? This is not a very easy question to answer because we can

quickly slip into anthropomorphism, or ascribing human-like qualities to animals without any evidence. But is there any evidence that dogs have a sense of humor?

From a personal standpoint, I can relate many stories of apparent sense of humor in dogs. When I played with my dog Raja, who loved to chase balls, he could sometimes invent games that made me laugh.

One game that he invented is pretending that he cannot find the ball. He will sometimes stand right over the ball and look all around as if he can't find it. He turns one way, then another way, all the time standing right over the ball. Then, suddenly, he "discovers" the ball that was touching his feet and grabs it.

He didn't do this all the time. Sometimes days or weeks went by before he would repeat this game, and then he might do it for several days straight until he apparently got bored with it and went back to running after the ball and retrieving it.

Another game that he invented was tripping on the way to get the ball. He would deliberately trip and slide about halfway to the ball, and then trip and slide about halfway back with the ball. This always reminded me of slapstick comedy, and I would break out in peals of laughter.

So how do I know that he thought it was humor? As he did this, he would start to pant rhythmically. At first, I noticed this behavior but did not realize that it had any sort of meaning. Then I read about studies of laughter in dogs. Dogs will produce a distinctive pattern of pants when they are playing, or when they are interacting with friendly people. This pattern is different from the panting that dogs do when they are hot or when they have been running.

I don't think that it is a large leap of faith to assume that if dogs can laugh, they can have a sense of humor.

HOW TO READ YOUR DOG

MOUTH

- Mouth closed, front of mouth puckered showing teeth: The dog is feeling aggressive.
- Mouth closed, but the entire lip of the mouth is puckered showing some teeth: The dog is scared.
- Mouth open, tongue lolling out: The dog is relaxed.
- Mouth somewhat open, making a rhythmic sound faster than panting: The dog is laughing.

4

FACES

When my dog Raja saw a strange dog, he had a very predictable response. His body tensed, he became rigid, and he stood very still, looking at the dog. As a puppy, he was abused by other dogs and even years later, he still had trust issues with dogs that he didn't know.

However, when he saw a dog he knew, even if a year or more had passed, his tail would start to wag and he confidently went up to the other dog as they happily started on dog-greeting protocols.

I have often wondered how he recognized and remembered the dogs he knew. Is it their smell? Is it their general size and shape? Is it the color of their coat?

While all of these factors probably play a role, studies have shown that dogs can recognize the faces of other dogs.

One study used a technique called visual paired comparison. In this technique, an animal is shown two images projected on screens, one to the right of the animal and the other to the left. Experimenters measured the amount of time that the animal spent looking at each image. If the dog had no preference, she would spend an equal amount of time looking at either image. However, if the dog had a distinct preference for one image over another, she would spend more time looking at that image.

The experimenters showed seven adult dogs (one miniature dachshund, two lurchers, and four mixed breeds) paired pictures of an unfamiliar dog face and a familiar one.

The dogs spent significantly more time looking at the familiar dog face. This means that dogs not only recognize individual dog faces but also prefer to look at familiar faces rather than strange ones.

In this respect, dogs are not alone. Increasingly, studies are finding that lots of other animals can recognize individual faces within their own species. So far, this list includes animals as diverse as chimpanzees, monkeys, sheep, cows, budgerigars, and paper wasps.

Dogs are sensitive to human faces as well. They can read the facial expressions of people and are drawn to people whose faces have a lot of expression. If a face doesn't have any expression, dogs quickly lose interest and go elsewhere.

They're particularly sensitive to smiles.

My dog Raja liked to sleep in during the morning. Hours after everyone in the house had gotten up, Raja was still asleep under his blanket, dead to the world. Eventually, he got up and walked around the house looking for people to say, "Good morning!" When I saw him coming down the hall, I would smile at him, reach out, and give him a morning massage while his tail wagged furiously. If I paid attention, I could see that he was smiling too.

I have always assumed that he was smiling because he loved the petting and the massage. It made me feel good to pet him, lowering my blood pressure, which already would be rising with the stress of the coming day.

But could he have been responding to my smile? If I were asked this question years ago, I would have answered, Of course not!

However, a study showed that dogs can indeed recognize the smiles of their people.

In their experiments, the researchers trained five dogs to respond to photographs of human faces. During the training phase, the dogs were shown two photographs: the smiling face of a university student and the back of that student's head. They were rewarded for choosing the photograph of the smiling face.

Then the experimenters showed each dog a photograph of their person's smiling face versus their person's face with a neutral expression, repeating this ten times with each dog. The dogs chose the photograph of the smiling person's face between 80 and 90 percent of the time, significantly above chance levels (chance would be choosing the smiling face and the neutral face 50 percent of the time each).

The experimenters then went one step further and showed the dogs photographs of the smiling faces and neutral faces of unfamiliar people of the same gender as the dogs' persons. Again the dogs chose the smiling faces between 70 and 90 percent of the time.

The last experiment turned out to be something of a puzzler. The experimenters showed the dogs both smiling and neutral photographs of faces of the opposite gender to the dogs' persons. Now the dogs fell to chance levels, suggesting that they couldn't tell the difference between the smiling face or the neutral face of someone with whom they weren't familiar. This last response suggests that it isn't just simple conditioning where the dogs have learned to respond to a smile, regardless of the face.

We can ask why. Maybe dogs have to learn that the smile on their person's face is associated with positive things, such as a food reward, a walk, or strokes. Or maybe dogs just feel good around their people and not as good around people they don't know. Maybe they feel particularly good when their person's emotion, expressed as a smile, washes over them. Clearly, we still have a lot to learn about this.

But I know one thing. I felt good when I saw Raja coming down the hallway, and I am pretty sure that Raja felt good when he saw me smiling.

5

DOGS BARKING AND GROWLING

One summer evening some neighbors came over for dinner. They are great dog people. They have rescue dogs and do all the right things in taking care of the dogs' ailments and infirmities.

That evening, as they sometimes do when they are not home, they left their dogs outside in a large run next to their house.

While we were having dinner, we could hear the dogs barking nonstop. My neighbors were surprised. They thought that the dogs would enjoy being outside. The weather was warm and balmy, the stars were out in glorious magnificence, and a gentle breeze blew whiffs of tangy vegetation. What's there for a dog not to like?

Dogs barking when left outside is a common problem. People often make judgments about what they think a dog would like and assume that a dog would like to be outdoors while they are gone. However, dogs are social animals, and when one of their pack is missing, they bark as a way of expressing their alarm and a way of reuniting the pack. If the dogs' people had been sitting outside on their porch next to the run, the dogs would not have been barking. But the people were missing, and so the dogs felt the need to bark as a way of expressing their agitation.

The same situation applies when people put their dog outside at night, and the dog barks or howls nonstop until morning. The dog feels separated from his pack and barks in alarm trying to get his people back. Besides, the night is often scary with strange noises and smells, and the dog may get frightened without the support of his pack members.

A distant neighbor down my street routinely puts his dog outside the minute it starts to get dark. And just as routinely, the dog starts to

bark. Fortunately, the dog is quite some distance from my house, so all I hear are faint barks, but these go on all night. If I get up in the middle of the night, the dog is still barking. If I get up before sunrise, the dog is still barking. I would have thought that this would drive the neighbor crazy, but he probably no longer even hears the barks.

In animal behavior, there is a principle called habituation. When a noise happens rhythmically, animals habituate to the noise and no longer hear it. I grew up in a house that had several wind-up, grand-father-like clocks that ticked loudly. Each ticked with its own rhythm, but they were slightly out of sync with each other—the ticking noise was constant. I didn't hear it. However, when I went away to college and then came back to my parents' house for holidays, I couldn't sleep. The ticking was driving me crazy. I can only assume that the immediate neighbors of the barking dog also habituated to the sound and no longer heard it.

In these cases, the solution is simple. Leave the dogs inside the house. When the dogs' people are gone, the dogs might still bark in alarm, but at least they have all of their familiar smells, food, and sleeping places where they can go to sleep. Sometimes leaving a radio or TV on will help pacify the dogs and help reassure them.

Where there is the potential for dogs to be destructive when left alone in the house, crate training could be the answer. A dog left inside a crate could feel secure and go to sleep as long as the dog has been familiarized to the crate through prior training, so the dog does not perceive having to go into its crate as a punishment. And it helps if the inside of the crate is comfortable and safe in its construction so that he can't chew of parts of it. If you're worried that it looks like your dog is in jail, just remember that his ancestors were used to sleeping inside a den.

In dealing with dog behavior problems, the important thing is to think like a dog.

While barking may seem like it's all the same sound and can annoy us, dogs actually incorporate a lot of information into their barks. One study looked at the responses of dogs to the recorded barks of another dog who was barking at either a stranger coming to the door or being left outside tethered to a tree. The experimenters measured the heart rate of the listening dogs as a way of determining the extent to which the dogs were influenced by the barks and could discriminate between the different situations. The barks to the stranger produced the highest changes in heart rate, but barks to the situation of being left alone outside also produced a significant response, indicating that the dog barks encoded information about these two different situations.

Another study looked at whether listening dogs could tell the difference between the barks of several individual dogs when these dogs were barking at a strange person and barking because they were left alone. Not surprisingly, the dogs in this experiment were able to correctly identify the different individual dogs who were barking in these two different contexts.

One study looked at the acoustic properties of the barks of a German shepherd in response to four different contexts: angry, crying, lonely, and happy. Using some sophisticated methods of voice analysis, the study found that the acoustic properties of dog barks for these four different contexts were different. We don't know at this point whether the dogs were able to detect these differences.

We do know, however, that a bark is not just a bark. A study looked at the barks of hunting dogs toward other species of animals and found that there were significant differences in the barks of the dogs toward four other animal species: wild boar, red fox, rabbit, and fowl. As we learn more about how to decipher dog barks, we will probably learn that dog barks contain a lot of information about the context of the bark, as well as the emotional state of the dog who is barking.

Barks are noisy signals. Unlike a pure tone, such as a note played on the violin, barks contain all kinds of sounds, more reminiscent of the lack of acoustic structure found in noise. Scientists have sometimes characterized barks as chaotic signals because of all of the different sound waves that are found within a bark.

Despite that, there are some generalities that can be found in dog barks. These generalities also apply to dog growls and to whines. In the communication system of many animals, including humans, there are distinct differences in the meaning of low-pitched sounds versus high-pitched sounds. Low-pitched sounds like deep growls or deep-voiced barks are usually signs of aggression. A dog that makes a sound like this can easily bite you. High-pitched sounds are usually signs of fear. A dog that makes a high-pitched bark or a whine can also bite you as a result of fear, but more likely the dog simply wants to run away. Barking at a stranger is often done with a low-pitched bark, while a dog that is left alone in the house and suffers from separation anxiety will vocalize with high-pitched whines and high-pitched barks.

The pitch can be combined with loudness to elaborate on the meaning. Loud low-pitched sounds are indicative of more threat and possibility of aggression than less-loud low-pitched sounds, and similarly, loud high-pitched sounds are indicative of more fear than softer sounds.

We seem to instinctively recognize these differences. One time I was walking in the desert at night where there were the shadows of small trees and bushes alongside my path. I had a flashlight and was paying attention to what was in front of me in case I came up to a rattlesnake, but I wasn't paying attention to what was going on to either side

of me. Suddenly, from behind a medium-sized bush on my right came a loud, deep-voiced growl. The biologist in me momentarily thought, this is really very interesting, I wonder who is making that growl, and maybe I should swing my flashlight over and see who it is. The human in me said, run like hell. And that's what I did.

The size of the dog determines to some extent whether the dog is capable of producing low-pitched barks. Some of the smaller breeds of dogs, like a chihuahua, produced relatively high-pitched barks even in contexts where they are feeling aggressive. This is simply a function of the size of their vocal tract. Perhaps for this reason people tend not to take the barks of small dogs very seriously and can get bitten in the process. Fortunately, small dogs also tend to have small teeth, but even the bite of a small dog can be serious.

Another factor in dog barks is the interval between the barks. Low-pitched barks that have a very short interval between them are generally given by dogs in an aggressive context, while medium-pitched barks with a longer interval between them are usually given in the context of asking for attention. Higher-pitched barks with a longer, variable interval between them are usually seen in the context of play.

Studies have found that people are not very good at discriminating between the contexts of different dog barks. However, they can tell whether a bark is a low-pitched one or a high-pitched one, and from that they can get some information about the general emotional state of the dog.

People are not very good at distinguishing between dog growls either. Let's say that your dog growls at you when you try to take away his food dish. Then he growls at you when you are playing tug with him. Can you tell the difference between the growls? Or does one growl sound like another to you?

It turns out, dogs can tell the difference between these two types of growls.

A study using forty-one dogs of various breeds tested whether dogs can tell the difference between growling when another dog approaches food, growling when an unfamiliar stranger approaches, and growling while playing tug.

The experimenters recorded dog growls in all three contexts. Then they played back the different growls to a dog approaching a bone. Here's how it was done: a dog was allowed to approach an untended bone, and when the dog's nose was close to the bone, the experimenters played back either a food-guarding growl, a threatening stranger growl, or a tug growl.

The results were striking. When the food-guarding growl was played, eleven of twelve dogs withdrew from the bone. Compare this with the other growls: two of twelve dogs withdrew from the bone when they heard the threatening stranger growl, and four of twelve dogs withdrew when they heard the play tug growl.

Clearly, the dogs understood the meaning of the growls.

All three types of growls had different acoustic properties in terms of pitch and places where the most sound energy was concentrated. The food-guarding growls and the threatening stranger growls were lower in pitch than the play tug growl.

One question that I often get from people is how to keep their dogs from barking. By the time that they talk to me, they have tried yelling things like "Stop barking!" or "Shut up!" which to their surprise has usually resulted in their dog barking even louder. Trying to yell even louder has not had any effect. As anyone who has been around a barking dog knows, dogs can bark louder and longer than people can yell.

I first explain that yelling at a barking dog does not do any good. The dog interprets the yelling as more barking and is pleased that the other pack members are finally joining in to sound the alarm. Yelling louder tells the dog that even more effort is needed, and so she redoubles her efforts.

Instead I suggest using a simple form of learning, based on the natural behavior of dogs. When a mother dog wants to discipline her pups, she will put her head on the pup's head and gently push down. At the same time, she might give a low growl.

This same behavior can be used to teach a dog not to bark. If your dog is barking, put one hand on the back of the neck of the dog and gently push down. The operative term here is "gently." Do not do anything that could injure your dog or cause her any physical discomfort. At the same time say, "Quiet!" in a low voice that sounds like a growl.

When your dog stops barking, say whatever words of praise that you normally use, in a high-pitched happy voice. I like to use "Good dog!" in a high-pitched voice. The high pitch is important because this is the tone that dog mothers use when they are pleased with their pups.

Repeat this situation whenever the dog is barking inappropriately. If the dog barks when she sees another dog, you can maybe have a friend walk their dog past yours a few times while you do the "Quiet!" routine.

Within a short while, the dog will learn to stop barking when you say, "Quiet!" With my dog, I like to have him bark a few times whenever someone rings the doorbell, and then I will say, "Quiet!" and he will stop, confident that I will handle the situation from that point on.

One caution, however, is to never do this when the dog is barking because of aggression or fear. When emotionally aroused, the dog can turn around and bite your hand. If you have the slightest doubt about the dog's possible response, don't do it. Leave it to a professional trainer—don't under any circumstances risk getting bitten.

Barking dogs can be very annoying, but with a little bit of patience and application of learning theory, dogs can learn to stop barking on command.

HOW TO LISTEN YOUR DOG

BARKS

- The dog has low-pitched barks, spaced close together: The dog is being aggressive.

- The dog has medium-pitched barks, spaced at longer intervals: The dog wants attention.

- The dog has high-pitched barks, spaced at regular intervals: The dog is frightened or separated from her people.

- The dog has short, high-pitched barks, spaced at irregular intervals: The dog wants to play.

HOW TO LISTEN YOUR DOG

GROWLS AND WHINES

- The dog has low-pitched sustained growls: The dog is feeling aggressive.

- The dog has short, low-pitched growls: The dog is playing.

- The dog has high-pitched irregularly spaced whines: The dog is happy, playing, or asking for attention.

- The dog has high-pitched regularly spaced whines: The dog is frightened or in pain.

6

DOGS AND A SENSE OF SMELL

How good is your sense of smell? Can you smell where someone walked by half an hour before? No? Most dogs can.

Dogs have an amazing sense of smell. Their nose has between 10,000 and 100,000 more receptors for odor than we do. If you look closely at a dog's nose, you will see that there are slits along the side of each nostril. These slits trap air that the dog has been breathing and maximize the contact of that air, amplifying what the dog is smelling in the immediate environment.

The things that dogs can do with their sense of smell are simply amazing. Lots of stories tell of bloodhounds that can track a person's scent days after the person was there. Dogs can be trained to smell the location of cancers on human bodies, and not only that, but they can also be trained to smell out different kinds of cancers. Dogs can smell whale poop from half a mile away, allowing researchers to locate otherwise invisible whales swimming below the ocean surface. And those of us who travel by air through airports are quite familiar with the friendly-looking beagles or similar-sized dogs who go around sniffing our carry-on luggage, looking for either drugs or explosives.

New evidence shows something that is hard to believe. The neural connections from smell in a dog's brain also go to the visual cortex. This raises the possibility that dogs can see odors. Lots of people have wondered how blind dogs can do things like catch frisbees or chase and retrieve balls that they can't see. But if they can see through their smell, they can smell the location of the frisbee or the ball and form a mental picture of all of the surroundings through their sense of smell.

If you have ever had the pleasure of having a dog express all the contents of her anal glands because she got scared, you are not likely to forget that experience. It smells horrible. But the anal glands contain a number of different chemicals that relate to the gender of the dog, the dog's physiological condition, the mood of the dog, and probably the age of the dog. Dogs can modify the ratio of these chemicals, just like we change the words in our sentences, providing fairly detailed information about themselves to other dogs. The anal gland secretions are expressed in small quantities when a dog poops. This is why dogs will stop and smell other dogs' poop when you take them for a walk. To us it seems gross. To the dogs it's just reading the news of the neighborhood.

Dogs seem to like odors that smell horrible to us. They sometimes like to roll around in dead roadkill or decaying plants. One time my dog Zephyr got sprayed by a skunk and then ran up to me. If you have ever smelled skunk odor up really close, you know that it has an acrid smell that is much stronger than the pungent skunk smell that comes from a skunk that was hit by a car. My wife and I washed Zephyr repeatedly and used up our entire supply of tomato paste in the hope of neutralizing the odor, and while it helped cut down the acrid smell, it still kept a very strong skunk smell that lasted about three weeks, gradually fading out. And Zephyr? He seemed to love it. Maybe to him, it was like putting some high-quality perfume on his fur. I wish we could have seen it that way.

We can't read the odors of dogs the way that we can read their visual and acoustic signals. The best we can do is say something like, my dog smells bad. Often we'll give our dog a bath, using soaps that smell good to us but probably don't smell that great to our dog, because not only have we given the dog an artificial scent, but we've also washed off a lot of the chemical odors that the dog uses to communicate with other dogs.

Unfortunately, we also can't talk to our dogs through odors. At least not yet. Various companies are working on ways of digitally synthesizing odors, and once we know more about what odors mean to dogs, we might be able to synthesize odors that mean specific things that a dog would recognize. For the time being, however, we are left with visual and auditory signals.

7

DOG TRAINING

While we are learning to talk to our dogs, we also must teach them how we expect them to behave. Just like all members of the family must learn some basic rules that make living in the family easier—think of teaching kids how to speak to adults and how to have good table manners—teaching dogs how to function in a family group is important.

One of the features that is important is to teach dogs some basic commands that make life easier for their people. This usually involves training the dogs, and training can involve a variety of methods.

DO CONFRONTATIONAL TRAINING METHODS WORK?

In my dog training classes, people often came to me and told me that they tried hitting their dog or yelling at him to stop a particular behavior, but nothing seemed to work. My response has always been that rewards are better than punishment. However, this was based on my own experience and on learning theory. All I had was anecdotal data and a conviction that dogs should not be treated this way.

However, one study surveyed 140 dog owners whose dogs had a variety of behavioral issues, such as aggression to familiar people, aggression to unfamiliar people, aggression to dogs, separation anxiety, or a variety of fears such as to thunderstorms and loud noises. The authors asked the owners to list the methods that they used to deal with these behavioral issues. The owners were also asked if they were bitten, snapped at, or growled at as a result of using these methods.

The methods that were used could be grouped into two categories: confrontational and nonconfrontational.

Confrontational methods were subdivided into direct confrontation and indirect confrontation.

Direct confrontation included the alpha roll (rolling the dog on his back), pushing the dog down into a lying position, hitting or kicking the dog, jabbing the neck, yanking on a prong or choke collar, using leash corrections, making the dog wear a muzzle, forcibly removing something from a dog's mouth, forcibly pulling the dog down with a leash, grabbing the dog by the scruff of the neck, fitting the dog with a shock collar, and rubbing the dog's nose in soiled areas.

Indirect confrontation included yelling "No," spraying the dog with a water pistol or bottle, growling at the dog, or staring down the dog.

Nonconfrontational methods included using the "Look" or "Watch Me" commands, food rewards, food-stuffed toys, use of food as a trade for an item that the dog is holding, using the "Sit" command, and clicker training.

Among the direct confrontational methods, many provoked an aggressive response (bite, snap, growl, bare the teeth, or lunge at a person) from some dogs. Each of the following direct confrontational methods is listed with the percent of dogs who responded with an aggressive response: hitting or kicking the dog, 43 percent; forcibly removing something from the dog's mouth, 38 percent; muzzle use, 36 percent; alpha roll, 31 percent; dominance down, 29 percent; grabbing the dog by the scruff of the neck, 26 percent; forcing the dog down with a leash, 17 percent; choke or pinch collar, 11 percent; and shock collar, 10 percent.

Indirect confrontational methods also provoked aggressive responses from some dogs. Each of the following indirect confrontational methods is listed with the percent of dogs who responded with an aggressive response: growl at the dog, 41 percent; stare down the dog, 30 percent; water pistol or bottle, 20 percent; and yelling "No," 15 percent.

Among the nonconfrontational methods, the percentage of dogs responding with aggression ranged from 0 to 6 percent. The highest aggressive response was when food was used as a trade for an object the dog held (6 percent). Using the "Look" or "Watch Me" commands and

using clicker training showed a 0 percent aggressive response, while using food rewards, the "Sit" command, and food-stuffed toys each had a 2 percent aggressive response.

The results of this survey show that using aggressive correction methods on a dog can result in an aggressive response. Some of this might be aggression as a result of fear on the part of the dog. An earlier published study reported that using punishment in training dogs can give rise to fear-related responses.

Interestingly enough, the dog owners were asked in the survey where they learned about the methods that they used.

Many owners reported learning about direct confrontation methods from dog trainers. The percent of owners who learned about these methods from trainers is as follows: force dog down with a leash, 70 percent; choke or pinch collar, 66 percent; leash correction, 50 percent; knee dog in the chest for jumping, 31 percent; bark-activated shock collar, 40 percent; remote-activated shock collar, 29 percent.

Use of many of the nonconfrontational methods fell into the category that the authors of the survey called "Self"; in other words, the owners thought of using these methods themselves, without any recommendations from anyone. The percent of owners who fell into the "Self" category for the different nonconfrontational methods is as follows: using food to trade for an item held by the dog, 63 percent; food rewards, 56 percent; using the "Sit" command, 54 percent; food-stuffed toys, 54 percent; "Look" or "Watch Me" commands, 34 percent; and clicker training, 23 percent. However, between 31 and 60 percent of the owners reported that these methods were also recommended by dog trainers.

The value of this study is that it presents quantitative data showing that rewards work better than punishment in training dogs.

CLICKER VERSUS VOICE TRAINING

In recent times, clicker training has become quite fashionable. And rightly so. Clicker training has a lot going for it. The basic principle is that dogs learn to associate the sound of a click with some kind of reward, and this association facilitates learning desired behaviors. For clickers to be effective, they have to be "biologically charged," meaning that initially the sound of the clicker has to be paired with something that is biologically meaningful to a dog, such as food. At the sound of the click, the dog is given a favorite treat, and over time the dog learns to associate the click with good things happening in her life. The click can then be used to reinforce desired behaviors, because the click becomes the reinforcer for the behavior through associative learning.

By judicious use of clickers, dogs can be taught a variety of behaviors. If the clickers are used correctly, it represents an easy way to teach good behaviors.

However, clickers have their downside as well. For one thing, a clicker is easily lost or misplaced, so that it may not available at all times and may not be on hand to reinforce behavior. And one of the key aspects of learning in dogs is to be consistent in behavioral reinforcement. Another downside is the timing issue. For clicker training to be effective, the sound of the click has to co-occur within a second of the presentation of the food reward during the "biological charging" phase and has to occur within a second of the performance of a desired behavior during the training phase. Too much time between the click and the reward and the dog will not associate the click with the reward. Similarly, too much time between the performance of the desired behavior and the click and the dog will not associate the behavior with the click.

Timing is everything, and many people have a lot of difficulty getting the timing to work correctly.

An alternative to clicker training is using the voice. Here the idea is that when a dog does something that is desired, the dog is reinforced by saying something like "Good dog!" in a high-pitched, happy-sounding voice. As with clicker training, biologically charging this is very desirable, by initially saying, "Good dog!" and giving the dog a food treat or other kind of reward that the dog likes.

There are a few advantages that voice training has over clickers. One advantage is that using a high-pitched, happy-sounding voice mimics the whine that dog mothers use with their puppies to reward the pups for correct behaviors, and dogs are predisposed to respond well to such sounds. Another advantage is that we usually always have our voices with us, while we might forget our clickers on the kitchen counter. A third advantage is that the time that it takes to say, "Good dog!" usually overlaps the desired behavior, making the timing issue less of a concern.

For example, when our standard poodle Zephyr was young, we would take him out to the dog run, where he would sniff around. When he finally lifted a leg to urinate, we'd joyfully call, "Good pee-pee, Zephyr!" Over time, Zephyr learned what "pee-pee" meant, so for the rest of his life, telling him "pee-pee, Zephyr" would immediately produce the desired response. This was great during road trip breaks and when we needed to be somewhere in a hurry.

A disadvantage of voice training is that it is sometimes difficult for people, particularly those with deep voices, to say, "Good dog!" in a high-pitched voice. Some people find it physically impossible, while others are too embarrassed by what their neighbors and friends would think to say something like that with the right pitch and happy note.

Ultimately, it comes down to being a matter of preference. In either case, timing is crucial, and if done right, either one will work. In my dog training classes, I have had great success in teaching most people to use their voice as a reinforcer for desired behaviors, and a number of people who started out using a clicker converted to using their voice once they lost their clicker in the laundry or at the kids' soccer game.

One of the great things about dogs is that they are so eager to learn from us, even when we are not the greatest of teachers.

JUST SAY NO TO YOUR DOG

In the training classes that I have taught, I have found that a number of people are reluctant to say, "No" to their dog. In my classes, I stress positive reinforcement and trying to make training fun for both dogs and people. Some people see that as meaning that they should always let their dogs do whatever they want and then reinforce only the desired behaviors. The hope is that eventually, the dog will only do the desired behaviors.

However, some behaviors are self-reinforcing (the behavior is its own reward), and dogs might not ever learn that some actions are off limits as far as people are concerned.

So I suggest looking to the behavior of dogs for a solution of how to set limits. When a dog doesn't want another dog to do something, the first thing the dog does is growl, using a low-pitched tone of voice. The other dog immediately understands that he is transgressing a limit, and unless he wants to push things and escalate the encounter, he should stop what he is doing.

We can do the same thing with our dogs, using natural dog behavior. If a dog is doing something that we don't want her to do, we can say, "No" in a low-pitched tone of voice. Actually, I prefer saying "Naaaaaah" in a low-pitched tone of voice, because that sounds more like a growl, rather than saying a sharp and short "No." I find that men, with their lower-pitched voices, have an easier time saying this than women, who tend to have higher-pitched voices. Conversely, women have an easier time mimicking the higher-pitched sounds that dog moms use to praise their pups, by saying, "Good dog!" in a high-pitched tone of voice.

The important point is to make the "Naaaaaah" sound in as low a pitch and as sharply as possible. This usually has the effect of pulling the dog up short from whatever she was doing, and once she stops, she can then be rewarded with either a high-pitched "Good dog!" or a clicker, or a food treat. Saying, "Naaaaah" sharply is different from yelling "No" to a dog, because the yelling is often associated with facial expressions that a dog might find intimidating.

Using the concept of "No" sets up a system where the dog learns about boundaries. Let me add that under no circumstances do I advocate yelling at the dog, hitting the dog, or otherwise abusing her. A simple application of natural dog behavior is more than enough to train a dog to be a well-behaved citizen at home or on the street.

ALTERNATIVE WAYS TO TRAIN DOGS

In my dog training classes, I use a combination of operant conditioning and Pavlovian conditioning to train the participants. Operant conditioning involves reinforcement for a correct behavior or response, and Pavlovian conditioning involves pairing two stimuli together so that the dog learns to link the two in her mind. For example, when I say, "Sit" and the dog sits, she gets a reward, either as a food treat or as praise. The sitting part and the reward are operant conditioning. And when I pair the word "Sit" with a hand signal for "Sit," that is Pavlovian conditioning because after enough repetitions, the dog learns to associate the hand signal with sitting and responds to it alone. This has been a tried-and-true method for training dogs.

However, there might be other ways of training dogs. One study tried training dogs with the model-rival method. The model-rival method has been used extensively by Irene Pepperberg in training her African grey parrot Alex to learn to recognize different shapes and different colors and to say the names of those shapes and colors when he was asked about them.

The basic method of the model-rival technique involves two people talking about an object in the presence of the animal. One person asks the other some question about the object, and the other person answers and is given the object if the answer is correct. Meanwhile, the animal observes the interaction. Then the animal is asked to join in by providing the correct answer.

In the case of dogs, two experimenters compared the results of using operant conditioning and using the model-rival technique in

training six male and three female dogs to retrieve an object that had a distinct name. In the model-rival part of the experiment, rubber toys that had a similar appearance were used. There were three red rubber toys (a boot, a fire extinguisher, and a strawberry) and three yellow rubber toys (a saxophone, a toothbrush, and a hammer). The experimenters chose a toy at random, and if it was a red one, they called it "Socks," and if it was a yellow one, they called it "Cross." Then, while a dog was tethered on a leash 0.5 meters (1.5 feet) away from them, the two experimenters had a conversation along these lines: "Can you see the Socks?" (handing the toy to the other person). "Yes, these are great Socks" (handing the toy back), and so forth for two minutes. Then the dog was told, "Go get the Socks," and the dog had to go and retrieve the object that the experimenters had called Socks from among the other two similar toys that did not have any labels.

In the operant conditioning part of the experiment, the dogs were trained to retrieve a single toy whose name was given, when no other toys were available. Here the experimenters used the standard tool of shaping, or rewarding, the dog at first if she came close to the object, and then later rewarding the dog for touching the object, and eventually only rewarding the dog for retrieving the object.

The experimenters found that the dogs on average learned to bring back the correct toy in the model-rival method as quickly as they learned to retrieve the toy with the operant conditioning method.

Another group repeated these studies and extended them somewhat. In addition to using the model-rival technique, these experimenters used a technique called direct enhancement, in which one person held the correct object in her hands and kept looking at it, while the other person spent the whole time looking at the dog. This study confirmed that the model-rival method worked well in training dogs to retrieve objects but also found that the direct enhancement method, where the experimenter spent the time looking at the object, worked as well as the model-rival technique.

What these results show is that there may be other ways to train dogs. Some of these ways might be better than what we are using today. In the model-rival method, the dogs actually learned the labels that were given to the objects that they were expected to retrieve. With operant conditioning, it is not clear whether they learned the labels for the objects or simply learned that a particular word (for example, Socks) stood for a food reward that they were given at the conclusion of their task.

These kinds of experiments suggest that dogs might be learning much more from us than we have given them credit for. Our theories about animal learning mostly come from laboratory rats that live their entire lives in cages. But our dogs are social, interacting creatures living in a rich world of experience, and it may well be that we have just begun to scratch the surface of their abilities to learn from us.

WHEN YOU ARE OUT AND ABOUT

One of the joys of being outside is walking with your dog. He is usually happy to have some exercise, sniff all of the outside smells, and generally enjoy the day. And you can delight in how happy you have made your dog.

Keep in mind that ideally, you and your dog are a team when you walk outside. Your dog looks to you for guidance and protection and will protect you if the need arises. There are lots of potential surprises any time you are outside together, and it's important to know your dog and be aware of her personality.

In public outdoor situations, you need to know if your dog is happy, upbeat, and confident, or if she is uncertain, wary, or sometimes even frightened, or proud, challenging, and aggressive. Knowing this will help you determine where it is best to take your dog. If you love art fairs and you have a dog with an uncertain and wary personality, it's not a good idea to suddenly expose her to thousands of legs, where her eyesight is hemmed in and her nose is swamped with tons of people odors. Yes, you can take a dog like that into crowded situations, but first you must build up her confidence and trust in you, so that she realizes that you, her teammate, will not put her into a harmful situation.

On many a morning, I went with my standard poodle Raja to a nearby state park that had a large pond, where we could see a variety of birds and other animals. Lots of other people also walked their dogs there, and state park rules mandated that every dog had to be on a leash. Raja was usually hesitant to approach other dogs, so I would swing wide around other people and their animals. We would exchange polite "Good mornings," and proceed on our way.

One time, however, coming toward us was a gentleman with a husky. I pulled Raja aside, but Raja started wagging his tail furiously and pulling on the leash. The husky did the same. I looked at the body language of both dogs and thought that everyone looked enthusiastic about a meet and greet.

I asked for permission to bring Raja up to the other dog. To my surprise, the person said, "She usually doesn't like other dogs. I wouldn't advise it." Not the answer that I was expecting. In my experience, most people answer with "Yes" even if their dog is snarling and showing his teeth. With that, all I could do was keep on walking in the opposite direction. As I walked, Raja kept turning his head toward the other dog, and she was doing the same to look at Raja.

I kept meeting them at the state park. It seemed that we were on the same schedule. Each time the scene would be repeated. Raja would wag his tail furiously and strain at the leash. So would the other dog. The dog's person would step away from us and keep going.

Finally, after about the tenth encounter, I said to the person, "Look, I know about dog behavior, and I can guarantee you that these dogs want to meet each other. I will take personal responsibility for anything bad that happens if you let your dog meet mine."

With great reluctance, he let me approach. Raja and the other dog, whose name turned out to be Kiva, were ecstatic. They went through all of the dog protocols of meeting another dog. Their tails were wagging mostly to their right, going full tilt. Clearly, they liked each other.

Seeing that his dog was not going to be attacked, the man was reassured. We started talking while our dogs were socializing, and it turned out that we had a lot in common. We both had taught at universities, he on the East Coast and I in Arizona. Our dogs had introduced each of us to a new friend.

After that, we made arrangements to meet at the state park on certain days at specific times, so that our dogs could walk together. Raja and Kiva happily walked side by side while Kiva's person and I talked about a variety of things. Everything turned out great because I was able to get an accurate reading on both dogs' attitudes ahead of time.

However, meeting another dog can be a challenge.

Let's say that you are walking with your dog, who is on a leash, along a narrow sidewalk or trail, and you see another person and their leashed dog coming toward you. What do you do?

The first thing is to use your knowledge of dog language to assess the situation. What are the signals that the oncoming dog is projecting? What is happening with the tail? What is happening with the mouth? The ears? The general body posture?

The next thing is to quickly assess the signals that your dog is sending. Does your dog seem eager to meet the other dog? Is she looking confident, or does she look frightened? Remember that your dog looks to you for support and reassurance, and the worst thing that you can do for your relationship with your dog is to put her into a situation where she is frightened or, even worse, physically harmed in some way.

If it looks like the other dog is aggressive, then it is best for you to take charge of your team—put your dog on a sit-stay as far away as possible along the side of the sidewalk or trail. You can also step in front of your dog to remove the sight line between the two dogs.

What if your dog is acting aggressively and straining at the leash to get to the other dog? Again, put your dog on a sit-stay if possible. If conditions don't allow this, try to move your dog away from the other dog and her person. Hold on to the leash as close as possible to where the leash attaches to your dog's harness. Keep glancing at the other team and check their body language. If your dog continues to behave aggressively, be sure to warn the other person, and, if necessary, try to move yourself between your dog and the other dog. Putting your dog on a sit-stay and either firmly but calmly talking to your dog and/or repeating the hand command for stay helps to guide his attention away from the immediate situation and back onto you. This way, you're reinforcing that you're the team leader in this situation and you have everything under control.

It's always important to get a sense of the other person's body language and how they seem to you. Remember that there's no law that says you have to let every dog come in contact with your dog. There's also no law that says you must let other people pet your dog, no matter how doggone cute she is. Your job is to protect your team member, stay safe yourself, and have a good time.

Should you decide to let your dog socialize with an oncoming dog, it is very important to keep the leash loose. People who are afraid of other dogs will often keep their dog on a tight leash, and that sends a negative signal to their dog—my person is worried, so I should be too, and I should try to protect my person. Tight leashes can lead to unpleasant encounters, for both you and your dog.

A while ago I was taking my standard poodle for a walk in the local park. As usual, I had him on an expandable leash, closed down to about four feet so that he could comfortably walk beside me. The trail went around a tall clump of bushes, and as we turned, we saw directly in front of us a lady walking her golden retriever, coming toward us. Her dog was on a six-foot leash and walking in the "heel" position. By the time we all stopped, the two dogs were practically nose to nose with each other.

Both dogs were startled and started to bark. Although I knew better, I pulled back on the leash from the surprise of the encounter, and the lady also pulled back on her dog's leash. The two dogs simultaneously lunged forward, ending up practically touching each other's heads and barking furiously.

After a few seconds, both dogs settled into a play mode, bowing on their front legs and twirling around. I was expecting this from my dog, but the lady with the golden retriever was not, and she quickly got tangled up in the leash that her dog managed to wrap around her legs three times until both she and he were completely immobile.

This shows the potential dangers of encounters between two leashed dogs. I have watched many interactions between two dogs that were on leashes when their people were approaching each other head-on. Typically, both people tend to tighten up on the leashes because they are afraid that the oncoming dog is not friendly. Dogs respond instinctively to a constriction around their necks and shoulders by surging ahead (which is why trying to pull a dog back into a "heel" position by tugging on a leash does not work). Both people start to pull more, causing each dog to strain even more at the leash.

As the dogs pull, the people start getting nervous and communicate this to their dogs through body language or voice. Now the dogs start getting nervous and can easily slip into a protective mode that can include aggression.

Pulling on the leashes also prevents the dogs from doing the normal dog protocols, the body language that they use when they meet another dog. Usually, upon greeting an unknown dog, a dog will not stare at the other dog but will come up to one side slowly, and eventually sniff the other dog's anus. When two dogs are straining at their leashes, they are looking directly at each other (a threat signal) and

are directly facing each other (another threat signal). It is no surprise that this could lead to a potentially aggressive encounter between two normally "friendly" dogs.

What if the dog's person says yes, my dog is friendly, you look at their dog and the dog is wagging his tail, the mouth is smiling, and the ears are in a neutral position? You look at your dog and your dog is happy as well. Then let the two dogs come up to each other. They will sniff their muzzles first, one dog approaching the other from slightly to one side, and then move to sniff each other's anuses. This is perfectly normal behavior because this is how they can learn about each other's health, reproductive status, and probably much more in an instant. Check to make sure that both their tails are wagging. If one dog starts feeling insecure in the interaction, he will normally sit down. This is a sign that you should end the interaction. Say, "Have a good day" to the other person and move on.

Another scenario is if you are walking somewhere with your dog on a leash and you encounter one or more dogs who are off leash. Do the same kind of thing: try to assess the intentions of the other dogs. Look at the signals that they are sending. If the dogs are sending friendly signals, then it is okay for you to let your dog meet them. If they are sending aggressive signals or are approaching so fast that your dog is getting nervous or frightened, then you must place yourself between them and your dog and call out sharply and loudly, "Go away!" And keep yelling at them until they go or until you see the dogs' person come in sight. Then it's perfectly appropriate for you to call out: "Would you please call off your dogs?" or "Please control your dog."

Where I live, people go walking in the woods all the time without leashing their dogs. Most of the time it works out fine. If your dog is off leash and comes across other dogs who are off leash, your dog can decide to either run up to the dogs and socialize with them or run to you for support. If that happens, the best thing is to hold your dog by her harness and yell "No" loudly at the other dogs if they approach. Usually there is a person nearby who can call her dogs to her if it looks like your dog is not having a good experience.

Most people who let their dogs run off leash have well-socialized dogs who know how to interact with other dogs that they meet. Keep in mind that if you let your dog run off leash, you potentially have relatively little control over her. That's why I suggest that you don't let your dog off leash until you've trained her on recall—that even if something she sees is intensely interesting, she feels she has an obligation to come back to her teammate when you say, "Come!" The most successful off-leash expeditions are where the dog and person keep in visual contact, literally watching out for each other.

Knowing dog language goes a long way toward having happy walks with your dog.

HOW DOG TRAINING IMITATES LIFE

In my experience of teaching dog training classes, many people initially find it difficult to understand the principles behind the training methods. But really, the methods of training dogs are based on the same principles that we all encounter in our lives.

One important principle is the clarity of communication. If we want someone to do something for us, the best way to accomplish this is to clearly state what it is that we want. Hinting, skirting the issue in roundabout ways, or trying to state our request as a question (Do you want to stop for a cup of coffee?) will not be as effective as simply stating

what we'd like. It is the same thing in dog training. If we clearly state a command, the dog will understand, provided that the initial training has been done to teach the dog the meaning of the command. A clearly stated "Sit" accomplishes more than a roundabout "Won't you please consider sitting?"

Another important principle is trust. We tend to respond well to people whom we trust. If these people tell us to do something, we are confident that they will not be leading us astray and will not turn on us and put us into a hurtful situation. And what do we do with the people that we don't trust? We either avoid them or, if we can't do that, we are very cautious about our actions around them. Similarly, dogs need to trust their people. They need to be able to know that their people will not hurt them or put them into scary situations. With trust in their people, dogs are willing to do a lot. Without trust, dogs are usually reluctant to do anything other than avoid the people that they don't trust, just as we tend to avoid the people that we don't trust.

Some time ago, my wife and I were friends with a person who worked at rehabbing injured animals. When we'd invite him over for dinner, our standard poodle Raja (who was normally very friendly) would grow very tense in this person's presence. Raja never barked or made any overt negative move, but he was on the alert all evening.

When we all sat down in the living room, Raja would come over to my wife and sit very close to her, facing this person and watching him very closely. It appeared that he didn't like the person, or at least didn't trust him. This mystified us. One of our theories was that this person might have had a bad incident with dogs in the past and was projecting some negative signals. Another was that he might have brought in some scent from the wild animals in his job. But my wife refused to discount Raja's assessment, and it slightly altered how open she was with our friend. This is not an unusual occurrence. Many people tend to trust the opinions of their dogs about people, and that trust is not often misplaced.

A third principle is rewards. While animal behaviorists and learning theorists talk about reinforcement (defined as anything that strengthens a behavior), much of dog and human behavior can be described as driven by rewards. We like to do things that give us rewards, whether those rewards are more money, good food, good friends, interesting partners, or toys to play with. We generally do not do well in an environment where we are punished, and we try to either avoid that kind of environment or become very stressed if we can't do anything about it. Similarly, dogs are usually happy to do things for rewards, whether the rewards are food, praise, strokes, or a chance to play with a favorite toy.

A fourth principle is sociality. We humans are social beings. We like to be around other people. We enjoy the company of our friends and sometimes our family. People who are isolated from other people often become depressed and fail to thrive. So it is as well with dogs. Dogs are social animals, and they like being around their friends and family. With dogs, family is usually either their pack or the humans that they live with, who become the functional pack. But dogs also have friends, and they like to be around their friends as well. Dogs who live rich social lives tend to be happy dogs, while dogs who are isolated, who are put out into the yard alone or locked up in the house all day by themselves, tend to be depressed and unhappy.

At the level of these principles, there are a lot of parallels between human behavior and dog training. With these principles, we learn as we are growing up how to do well in the world around us, and once we have learned that, we apply these principles to most of our interactions with other people. Dog training is based on these same principles.

While there are a lot of details that go into training dogs (for example, getting the timing right between saying the command and responding with praise, either with voice or a clicker, when the dog obeys the command), and these details are best taught by experienced teachers, without these principles the training is going to fail, and both the dog and her people will be very unhappy in their relationship.

DOG NAMES

When you talk to your dog over the course of her life, the one word you will use most is her name. That's something to keep in mind when choosing a name for your dog. A lot of people ask me what name they should pick for their puppy. I tell them that while this is a matter of personal choice, there are some "dos" and "don'ts" in picking dog names. Let me first say that in 2022 the five most popular names for male puppies were Max, Charlie, Cooper, Milo, and Buddy. The five most popular names for female puppies were Luna, Bella, Daisy, Lucy, and Lily. For a complete list of the most popular dog names, see rover.com/blog/dog-names.

Here are some "dos" in picking a name. Pick a name that is short and easy to say. Pick a name that cannot be shortened to something that would embarrass you and your dog. Pick a name that has enough consonants and vowels to be carried over a long distance if you need to call your dog when he is far away from you.

Let me give you an example. My standard poodle's name was Raja. This was the name given to him by his original people. Subsequently, he went to a person who renamed him Rumpus. The latter name shortens to either Rump or Pus, neither of which has great connotations if you are yelling in the park for your dog to come to you. When I got Raja, I renamed him to his original name, and he learned to respond to it quickly. Raja is a name that carries well over wind or noise and is short enough that it is easy to pronounce. It also captured his princely and proud bearing, reinforcing in the minds of all who stopped to pet him that here is a stately dog.

There are some "don'ts" in picking a name. Don't pick a name that is either long or unpronounceable. If the name is too long, you will tend not to use it and perhaps come up with a variety of nicknames

that will only serve to confuse your dog. In dog training, consistency is the key, and if you say, "Here, Chuckles" one time and "Love, come here" another time, your dog will never learn his name, much less learn to come to you. In my experience, just like we like to hear someone say our name, dogs seem to like to hear their names, particularly when they are being praised. So it is important to be able to say, "Good dog, Buddy!" consistently.

Another "don't" is to pick an aggressive-sounding name, like Killer, Terror, Fang, Fighter, or something similar. In my experience, people who give their dogs such names sometimes expect their dogs to be aggressive, and the dogs seem to pick up on that expectation and act accordingly. As a young person in Chicago, my wife would have to walk by a certain house if she wanted to visit her friend. That house was set back from the street and had a large front yard ending in a chain link fence that bordered the sidewalk. As she walked past, the two resident dogs would leave the house and tear across the length of the yard and throw themselves at the fence, barking like mad. Their names? Crunch and Bandito. Well, what could you expect?

I have had clients who have bought dogs for protection and named the dogs with aggressive-sounding names, only to find that they soon needed protection from their dogs. I have recommended a name change (for example, Terror becomes Maxie) along with behavioral modification, and after a while, we would come up with a kinder, gentler dog, who would still protect his people should the need arise. However, I must stress that if you find yourself in this position, you must seek the advice of a qualified animal behavior professional who can see your dog and evaluate the circumstances.

Beyond these "dos" and "don'ts," dog names are a matter of personal preference. Personally, I prefer a name that is different and distinctive and captures some positive aspect of the dog's personality. But if you pick a name that you can say with joy and gladness, your dog will be very happy.

IMPRINTING AND DOG AGGRESSION

Not too long ago, one of my friends mentioned that she had heard about problems at a dog park. It seems that someone was bringing an aggressive dog who was trying to pick fights with the other dogs. The people who brought their dogs regularly to the park were up in arms. Talking to the aggressive dog's person was proving to be useless, because his attitude was that dogs should be able to work these things out among themselves, and he was not going to intervene in something that he saw as normal dog behavior. The owners of the smaller dogs were particularly terrified. The aggressive dog was big and could potentially hurt a little dog. No one knew what to do to solve this problem.

I said that I have seen such dogs before. In my experience, a dog who is aggressive toward other dogs has not been socialized properly. This often happens when people get a puppy who is four to five weeks old, before the puppy has had a chance to imprint on other dogs.

Imprinting is a form of learning that happens at an early age and lasts the lifetime of the animal. The first person to thoroughly investigate

the imprinting process was the Austrian ethologist Konrad Lorenz, who won the Nobel Prize in 1973 for his contributions to animal behavior. Imprinting takes place during a relatively brief period of time called the sensitive period, after which the information learned during the imprinting process either cannot be or is very difficult to reverse.

Lorenz found that ducklings and geese have a sensitive period shortly after hatching, where they respond to visual and auditory cues by following whatever object is making sounds. Usually that is their mother. In ducks and chickens, this sensitive period is somewhere between twelve and forty-eight hours after they hatch. Through this kind of imprinting, birds learn who their mothers are, and ducks, geese, and quail learn to follow their moms.

The following response is not limited to birds. Imprinting has been shown in a number of mammals as well. The nursery rhyme "Mary had a little lamb / Its fleece was white as snow / And everywhere that Mary went / The lamb was sure to go" describes a lamb who was imprinted on Mary.

But another important feature of imprinting is learning what species an animal belongs to, and whom to mate with in the future. This phase of imprinting is sometimes known as sexual imprinting. Among social animals, the imprinting tells a young animal not only who its future mating partner is likely to be but also whom to socialize with when the animal starts to grow up.

With birds, such imprinting can be a problem when someone takes a young bird out of a nest and the youngster imprints on humans. I know a person who rescues birds. She has a turkey vulture that she cannot release back into the wild because the vulture imprinted on humans at an early age, apparently because someone took him out of his nest and raised him. Now the vulture thinks that he is human and directs his courtship behavior at people instead of at vultures. Vulture courtship behavior includes, in part, regurgitating the rotten food that he has eaten, at the feet of his intended beloved.

Dogs go through an imprinting process too. In dogs, the sensitive period lasts roughly between a puppy's fourth and twelfth weeks of life. During that time, puppies learn who their mother is and also learn about future mates and their social group.

If a puppy is taken away from her mother at week four or five, she does not have a chance to imprint on dogs as social partners. She does imprint on people, and subsequently she thinks of herself as a person rather than as a dog. So when she is placed in the company of other

dogs, she has neither the social skills to know how to interact with them nor even very much interest in going through dog greeting protocols. She sees herself surrounded by alien beings and responds aggressively.

Fortunately for the dog-human bond, dogs can imprint on both dogs and people during the sensitive period of imprinting. If a dog is allowed to be with his mother and littermates from about week four to about week eight, he will imprint on dogs and will learn dog social skills. If the dog is then placed in the company of people during weeks eight through twelve, he will imprint on the people that he sees around him.

While the effects of imprinting can sometimes be reversed, it takes a lot of work. A dog who was not imprinted on other dogs at an early age can be socialized, but it requires a lot of patience and effort on the part of the dog's people.

A much better solution is to let puppies imprint on other dogs at an early age and only take them away from their mothers and littermates when they are around eight weeks old.

8

DOG EMOTIONS

Dogs can have strong emotions.

One evening my dog Raja was invited for the first time to the home of a friend, a dog with whom we walked almost every day. Raja was very excited. At last, he would have a chance to play all evening.

When we arrived, Raja's friend was excited too. But she quickly cooled her excitement when Raja started playing with her toys and lying down on her bed mat. She went off to lie down at her people's feet and snarled when Raja came close.

Raja was dejected. His tail drooped, his head hung down, and he kept coming up to us and nudging our hands, seeking reassurance. When it was time to go home, Raja's friend did not get up from where she was lying and did not even wag her tail in farewell.

The next day, Raja was clearly depressed. He spent most of the day sleeping and could not even be roused for a game of fetch, one of his favorite games. The following day, I took Raja out for his daily walk where he usually met his friend, only to find that she did not want to come up to him, much less give him the enthusiastic greeting that he always received before.

Raja seemed devastated. During the entire walk, he had his head hung low and showed none of the symptoms of being a bouncy dog who loves his walks. Fortunately, the following day, when we met up with his friend, she greeted him with the usual affection, and Raja was transformed back into the happy, bouncy dog that he was before our visit to his friend's house.

What was happening here? Was Raja experiencing a variety of emotions similar to what we might feel when we have been rejected by a friend? Was his friend experiencing emotions of anger that Raja was playing with her toys and experiencing jealousy because Raja was getting praise from her people?

I think that the answer is clearly "Yes!" Raja was feeling badly because he expected to have a good time and instead was rejected. While some scientists would scoff at this and say that dogs are not capable of experiencing emotions, the bulk of the evidence seems to show that dogs, as well as other animals, can experience at least the basic emotions of fear, anger, joy, sadness, disgust, and surprise, and probably the same gamut of emotions that we experience.

Raja lived with my standard poodle Zephyr. A few years ago, I was walking with Zephyr and Raja along a dirt road in the desert. Because I was always concerned about the dogs finding rattlesnakes and being too inquisitive, I had them both on twenty-five-foot expandable leashes.

Raja always played the role of leader dog, the one who always had to be out in front when we walked. This did not translate into the traditional dominance idea, because in everything else he always deferred to Zephyr, who as an older, larger dog had never shown any aggression toward Raja.

In fact, Zephyr was a very sweet dog who wouldn't hurt a fly. He was my zoologist dog, interested in any animal that moved or flew. He often stopped to look at lizards and snakes, and insects fascinated him. He would stand and watch bees buzzing around flowers and would move around so that he could get a better view of them if his view was obstructed. Raja was more interested in being out in front of everyone on walks. Like Zephyr, he was very visual, but probably due to his challenging past, he was more alert and watchful for danger.

The dirt road that we were walking along had a lot of curves and dips, so it was hard to see more than one hundred feet ahead or behind us. I was in a semimeditative state, enjoying the warmth of the day, the blue sky, and the wind on my face. I was letting the dogs explore the general environment on their own, within the confines of the twenty-five-foot leashes, and was not paying that much attention to what was going on around me. Let me tell you that when you are walking around in the desert, it is always a mistake to not be aware of everything that is going on, what some people call situational awareness.

Suddenly from behind us came a rottweiler mix, running as fast as he could. Without any barking or growling, he lunged at Zephyr and tried to bite him on the back of the neck. Zephyr, who had never been in an aggressive situation, stopped, looking stunned.

I yelled. Raja, who was out in front about twenty-five feet from Zephyr, turned and looked at us. Instantly, without any hesitation, he ran full-tilt at the 120-pound rottweiler mix and slammed into him with his forty-pound body. This knocked the rottweiler back, giving me time to get between the dogs and the attacker. I had my hiking stick, which I poked at the attacker's face.

Around that time a pickup truck came driving up, with a man inside calling for his dog. The dog broke off the attack and came up to the truck. It seems that the man was using the lazy way to walk his dog, letting the dog run ahead while he drove behind.

I yelled at the man to control his dog. In addition, I had some choice words to say about people who let aggressive dogs run free, but I won't repeat those words here.

As often happens in such situations, the man was telling me that his dog had never done this before, and he couldn't understand why his dog would do that. Sadly, that is a common excuse that people use to justify the actions of their aggressive dogs, ignoring of course all the other times that the dog lunged at or tried to bite someone.

After making sure that the dog was safely locked up in the cab of the pickup, checking Zephyr (fortunately, he only had a scratch, thanks to Raja's quick action), and taking the man's name and phone number in case there was a problem with my dog, I tried to explain to the man that there could have been serious consequences. For one thing, in the desert, many people have guns, and someone could have shot his dog.

The man was unimpressed and left.

So why did Raja respond by attacking a dog who was much larger and much fiercer than he? If I toe the scientific line, I could go into a huge explanation about stimulus and response, and that perhaps Raja was conditioned at some point in his life to respond to certain cues with aggression. With this explanation, Raja mindlessly responded to the motion and size of the other dog.

However, I prefer another explanation. I think that Raja realized that his companion was in danger and selflessly threw himself into the fray to help out a friend whom he loved. Just like you and I might do in similar circumstances.

On another occasion, our cat Seri was bitten by a spider, probably a brown recluse. We knew that something was wrong when she disappeared under the bed and would not come out, mewing piteously on occasion. The next day she was still under the bed and would not come out to eat, something that was pretty unusual for her, because she was a social cat.

That evening I finally managed to extract her from under the bed to see what was wrong. Careful inspection revealed a characteristic spider bite, a large red ring enclosing dead tissue, with specks of blood throughout the affected area. Most spiders are only mildly poisonous and produce a small itchy lump if they bite. Brown recluse spiders, on the other hand, are quite poisonous, and their bites can sometimes leave

large areas of dead tissue in people who have been bitten. The spiders don't go out of their way to bite and try to run away if they can, but when they are squished by a cat paw or by an unwary human hand, they bite.

The next morning I managed to get an appointment with our veterinarian and put Seri into a cat carrier so that I could take her in to be evaluated.

During the whole time that Seri was under the bed, Raja kept sitting by the edge of the bed and would not move except to eat or go outside briefly. When I put Seri in the cat carrier, Raja was right there, nuzzling the carrier and whining softly.

As the time of the appointment neared, I put Seri into the car, preparing to go. Raja, who usually was very obedient about waiting at doorways to get permission to go through, ran past me to the car and jumped in through the open door. Because it was already a hot day, and I could not take him with me to the vet's office, I told him to get out.

He did, reluctantly. But then he would not go back into the house. He kept running around the car and ignored my demands that he go inside. Finally, I had to lift up all forty pounds of poodle and carry him into the house. He parked himself by the front door and would not leave that spot.

The vet confirmed that Seri had been bitten by a spider, gave me some antibiotic drops, and assured me that the bite should clear up within a couple of weeks.

Raja was overjoyed when I returned with Seri. As I took her out of the cat carrier, he kept trying to nuzzle her, to the point where she was starting to get irritated. When I released her, she ran under the bed, and Raja took up his position by the bedside.

Within a couple of days, Seri started getting better, whether from the antibiotic drops or from the green tea compresses that we were applying, and Raja became much more relaxed.

During the time that Seri was feeling poorly, Raja was acting like a concerned parent whose child was sick. As I think about this, I can put on my scientific hat and say that this is all anecdotal information that proves nothing. Or I can put on my hat as someone who believes that dogs have strong emotions and have great concern for their fellow beings who inhabit their houses. Of these two alternatives, I prefer the emotional one.

Studies have shown that dogs recognize the emotions of both humans and other dogs. One study showed dogs both human and dog faces that had either happy or angry expressions, and these were paired with either a happy or an angry vocalization from a dog. The experimental dogs looked significantly longer at both dog and human faces that matched the happy or angry vocalization, showing that dogs can discriminate between different emotions from either humans or from dogs.

Dogs can also assess the reputations of individual people, with perhaps a sense of justice. We all know someone who has a bad reputation. Backstabber. Malicious gossip. Liar. Cheater. Gets unpredictably angry. And we try to keep that reputation in mind when we deal with the person. If you are like me, you might give the person the benefit of the doubt, but then when it happens to you, you back off and are no longer willing to trust the person. As the saying goes, once bitten, twice shy.

But can dogs assess who has a bad reputation? On the surface, it might seem easy to give the knee-jerk reaction—of course not. Dogs are supposed to be friendly toward everyone and are supposed to lack the thinking skills that would allow them to form a judgment about reputations.

Not so fast, however, with the easy answers.

One study shows that dogs can make some pretty good judgments about people's reputations.

The experimenters used a very clever trick. While a dog was watching, they had two people kneeling side by side in front of another person who was kneeling facing the other two. The two kneeling people each gave the person facing them a treat by placing the treat in front of the person. But one of the two givers consistently took the treat back, while the other giver allowed the person in front of them to take the treat. Then each of the givers simultaneously offered the dog a treat by placing the treat in front of them, just like they did when they were offering the treat to the person. The dog was allowed to choose whose treat to take.

All ten dogs in this experiment chose to take the treat from the giver who didn't take back the treat.

To control for unintentional cues, the experimenters tried a variety of modifications of this experimental design, each with about ten new dogs. In one modification, the givers were kneeling facing away from

the recipient person and had to reach backward to offer the treat. In another modification, the givers were not people but large cardboard boxes with people inside reaching out to put down the treats. In a third modification, the recipient was a cardboard box.

In each case, at least nine of the ten dogs chose to take the treat from the giver who didn't initially take the treat back.

The experimenters concluded that the dogs formed a concept of the reputation of each of the givers: one giver was reliable in offering the treat, while the other one was unreliable.

Let's extend these results to our dogs. How many times have you yelled at your dog, hit your dog, yanked your dog by the collar or leash, or otherwise acted in an unpleasant manner toward your dog (my hope is that your answer is "zero")? For those who do that, these experiments imply that dogs are forming a concept of the reputation of their people.

Just as we don't do well in an environment of working with a boss who has a reputation for being unpleasant, maybe dogs don't do well living with people who have a reputation for being unpredictable.

And maybe dogs act out when they get the concept that the person that they are living with has a bad reputation.

The moral of the story—be nice to your dogs.

9

THINGS WE DON'T KNOW ABOUT DOGS

There are a number of things that we still don't know about dogs. Some abilities that have long been suspected, such as dogs being able to navigate by using the Earth's magnetic field, are turning up as people spend more time trying to find out more about dogs. Then there are scraps of information, not supported by scientific experiments, that hint at other senses and abilities of dogs that we either think that they might have or we are baffled at trying to explain. These fall into the category that scientists call anecdotal information, which usually means that scientists are not prepared to believe them.

I'll tell you two anecdotal stories about dog abilities, for which I have no reasonable explanation.

A number of years ago, I was living in a house that had a small enclosed porch in front of the main door. The porch had a screen door that I usually kept locked. When someone came to the door, they would ring the doorbell and I would go out on the porch, greet them, and unlock the screen door to let them in. My smooth collie mix Nenkin would usually accompany me out on the porch. She loved people and loved to say hello to anyone coming in.

One summer evening the doorbell rang and I went out on the porch. Standing in front of the screen door was a clean-cut man in his thirties. He explained that his car had broken down and asked if he could come inside to use our phone. This was prior to the general availability of cell phones, so his request sounded reasonable.

As I was about to unlock the screen door, Nenkin appeared at my side. She took one look at the man, and her hackles rose. She bared her

teeth and started to bark furiously. I couldn't believe that this was the same dog who lavished love on everyone coming into the house.

I grabbed her collar to keep her from lunging at the screen door and regretfully explained to the man that I was sorry, but I couldn't let him in because there was something wrong with my dog. He was clearly frightened by Nenkin's barking and went away quickly.

The next day I read about this man in our local newspaper. It seems that he went a couple of blocks down the street, knocked on a door with the same story, and a kindly elderly couple let him into their house. He overpowered them, tied them up into chairs, robbed the house, and stole their car. He was stopped for speeding some 150 miles away, and because his name did not match the car's registration, the police became suspicious and detained him. They called our local police department, asking an officer to check on the car's registered owners. Because there was no response to a phone call, an officer went to the residence of the elderly couple, found them tied up, and set them free. Without this chain of events, the couple could have died before anyone found them.

Somehow, my dog sensed that this was not a good person and saved us from possibly having the man rob us.

Was she psychic? Maybe.

But there might be an alternative explanation. Recent research is showing that dogs are very attentive to human body language and very subtle cues that we humans don't even notice. Perhaps there was something about the man's posture that gave him away. Or perhaps Nenkin smelled a scent of fear from the man, or a scent of rage. I never saw her do this behavior again toward anyone else.

Whatever it was, I was very grateful to her. Psychic or not, she saved the day.

The next story was told to me by a friend. She lives in a rural area where there are relatively few houses, surrounded by woods.

Some time back, she, her husband, and their dog were doing their usual morning walk in the woods. Just as they were about to go home, their black rottweiler/lab mix dog ran off. They called and called, but the dog was nowhere to be found.

They went home, thinking that the dog would be waiting for them by their front door. But the dog was not there. Because the dog wore a collar that had tags with their phone number, they hoped that someone would find the dog and would soon call.

Not too much later in the morning, their phone rang. The caller had found their dog and asked them to come.

When they came for the dog, the caller had a story to tell.

He was out alone, walking in the woods about four miles away from where my friend was walking with her dog. He stopped near a pine tree and was startled to see a mountain lion on one of the lower branches, crouched and ready to pounce.

Suddenly, a large black dog ran up, positioned himself between the man and the tree, and began barking at the mountain lion. Then the dog started to herd the man toward his truck, always keeping himself between the mountain lion and the man.

When they got to the truck, the dog jumped in and settled down into the passenger seat. The man drove back to his house and called my friend and her husband to come and get their large, black, rottweiler/lab dog.

But the story does not end there. The man explained that he was a Native American shaman and had had a dream several nights before that he was attacked by a mountain lion and was saved by a large black dog. He kept thanking the dog for saving him.

In terms of time, the dog would have had to run the entire distance in a straight line to reach the man and the mountain lion when he did.

And having herded the man back to his truck, the dog was quite happy to be taken home.

Was it just a coincidence? Or was it something else? We don't know.

Homing is another strange thing that we don't understand about dogs. Homing is the ability to find your way home after you have been displaced for some distance. Some of the champions of homing behavior are homing pigeons, who can be taken hundreds of miles from their home loft to a location that is not familiar to them. They are released and find their way home in a relatively short period of time. How they do that is not clear, but it might be due to the ability of the pigeons to sense the Earth's magnetic field and follow magnetic lines.

You can best see this if you think of a bar magnet around which you sprinkle iron filings. The filings will line up in an oval shape around the magnet. At the poles the filings will be oriented in an up–down direction, while around the middle of the magnet the filings will be oriented parallel to the body of the magnet. The magnetic field is oriented so that the lines of magnetic force curve upward at what we can call the south pole of the magnet and curve downward at what we can call the north pole. They are flat along what might be considered the magnet's equator or middle.

The same thing happens with the Earth's magnetic field. Lines of magnetic force point down at the north pole and point up at the south pole, while at the equator, they are flat. Homing pigeons and birds that migrate are believed to detect and rely on these lines of magnetic force to find their location. If the magnetic lines are curving down, they are flying toward the north pole. If the magnetic lines are curving up, they are flying toward the south pole. If they are flat, they are flying along the equator.

But the strength of the magnetic field fluctuates depending on local conditions, such as the amount of iron deposits in any one place. This creates the equivalent of a topographic map of magnetic field fluctuations, and homing pigeons and other birds are able to use the fluctuations as a way of orienting themselves to where they are. They can get lost if the fluctuations are too strong, such as around Sedona,

Arizona, where there are a lot of iron deposits and the magnetic field is unusually strong.

Recently, dogs have been found to be sensitive to magnetic fields. One study showed that dogs align themselves in a north-south direction when they poop. This has been suggested as a possible mechanism for how dogs might have a homing response when they are displaced to a location they don't know.

There are many examples of dogs having a homing response. One of the best-documented cases comes from Bobbie the Wonder Dog, a Scotch collie/English shepherd mix. Bobbie lived in Silverton, Oregon, in the 1920s with his people, Frank and Elizabeth Brazier.

While the Braziers were visiting their relatives in Wolcott, Indiana, Bobbie was attacked by three dogs and ran away. Although people searched for him, he was nowhere to be found. The Braziers returned to Oregon and reconciled themselves to having lost their dog. Six months later, Bobbie came back home to Silverton, dirty, thin, with sore feet. He had walked some 2,500 miles, crossing rivers and going across the Continental Divide in the dead of winter.

Because his story drew national attention, people who either saw Bobbie on his journey or helped feed him wrote the Braziers to tell

them where and when they saw him, so that his route across much of the United States could be traced. However, no one could say definitively how Bobbie figured out how to find his home.

Another story is reported by Dr. Stanley Coren in his *Psychology Today* blog post, "Do Dogs Have a Homing Instinct They Can Use If They Are Lost?"

Dr. Coren reports the story of Marin, a Shetland sheepdog, who lived in Los Angeles. In 1991 Marin's person, Rita, drove to San Francisco, taking Marin with her. Some twenty miles south of San Francisco, she stopped to phone her friends to say that she would be arriving soon. While she was on the telephone in a store or building, someone stole Rita's car, with Marin still inside. Later, her car was found in San Francisco, but Marin was gone. Rita had to come home to Los Angeles without her dog. Some five months later, Rita noticed that a dog was whimpering outside her door. She looked and saw a shaggy gray dog with bloody feet. Taking pity on the dog, she took the dog inside and gave the dog a bath. Once the dog was clean, Rita recognized that it was Marin, returning home after a journey of five months and three hundred miles.

A possible explanation for this is that Marin knew where home was and could use a sense of the magnetic field to find the way back to Rita.

A further story is more puzzling.

This is the story of Sally, as reported by J. Allen Boone in his book *Adventures in Kinship with All Life*. Sally was a sheepdog who lived on a farm in southern Arkansas. She and her people, an elderly couple, were inseparable. One day, the elderly couple decided that farm life was too strenuous for them and they needed to go on a retreat to a health center located in the mountains of southern California, far off the beaten track. Sadly, they felt that they couldn't take Sally with them and left her on the farm.

One day, three months after they came to the resort, they were sitting on the porch of their cabin, when they saw an exhausted dog, limping with bloody feet, approaching them and weakly waving her tail. It was Sally. Somehow she had crossed some 1,700 miles in the space of three months to find her people.

However, that is not the most puzzling part of the story. Sally had never been to the mountain retreat in southern California. She could not have used a compass sense to get there, because she hadn't been "there" to start with.

How did Sally know where to find her people? We have no clue.

Over shorter distances, dogs might use smell to find their way.

One time my wife took our standard poodle Zephyr out for a walk. She wanted to walk in the forest, among pine trees with their delicious scent. She piled Zephyr into the car and drove some thirty miles along dirt roads in northern Arizona until she found what she thought was the perfect spot for a walk. Pulling off the road, she decided to do some off-leash training with Zephyr. They would practice by walking a few minutes on leash, then she'd let Zephyr run free for a bit, and then she'd call him back to her. She would lavish him with praise and petting, then repeat the process. This went on for about twenty minutes as she and Zephyr explored a new area of dense pine forest.

All was well until Zephyr saw an elk. Off he went. Soon he was completely out of sight. My wife called and called his name, to no avail. She started going in the direction that he disappeared, hoping that he would hear her.

Soon she got lost. In a pine forest in the middle of nowhere, all the trees look the same and it's difficult to see the position of the sun. She thought, this is a fine fix. Not only have I lost our dog, but I am lost as well. Because she was used to wandering around in forests, she hadn't told anyone where she was going and didn't have a cell phone. Searching for her would have been useless because she could have been anywhere.

She decided to backtrack her route as best she could. After some minutes of walking, she came across a rough, unpaved old logging road and continued along that. Eventually, she heard the sound of a car in the distance and was relieved that at least she was walking in the right direction toward the road that she used to get there.

Then she came across that road. However, she had no idea whether her car was to the right of her or to the left. Relying on her usually good sense of direction, she chose to go to the right. After some ten minutes of walking, she finally made out the shape of a car pulled off the road. It was probably hers but still she was bereft. How would she ever explain that she had lost our precious dog? How would we ever find him in a wilderness that went on for more than twenty miles?

And then she saw Zephyr. He was sitting next to the car. After he lost the elk in the woods, he used his keen sense of smell to find the car and was sitting there patiently waiting for my wife to show up for their next adventure. As she trudged tiredly along, Zephyr hesitantly approached her. He seemed to know he was in big trouble. But she knew how lucky she was, so she gathered him into her arms and held him close. Luck was with both of them that day—my wife for choosing to go in the right direction, and Zephyr for being able to detect the smell of the car.

One strange attribute of dogs has been explored by Rupert Sheldrake, who presents his results in the book *Dogs That Know When Their Owners Are Coming Home*. Sheldrake had received a number of comments from people that their dog seemed to know when they were about to come home and would run up to the front door and wait for

them. He decided to do surveys of dogs' people to see if a large sample size would report this effect. He asked friends and people who attended his lectures to report to him whether they had observed their dog engaging in this behavior. In a series of informal surveys, he found that about one-third to two-thirds of the people responding had observed this behavior.

He decided to do more formal surveys. He and his associates randomly phoned people in four locations: North London; Ramsbottom, England; Santa Cruz, California; and Los Angeles. Of course, not everyone had dogs. In Santa Cruz and Los Angeles, 35 percent of the people sampled had dogs. In Ramsbottom it was 31 percent, and in North London it was 16 percent.

Of the people who had dogs, about 50 percent said that their dogs anticipated their return. Typically, the dogs would start running to the front door around ten minutes before their person returned, although some people reported that it was more like sixteen to twenty-five minutes.

Why only a 50 percent response, if this is a common phenomenon among dogs? Sheldrake offers some suggestions. Obviously, someone else has to be home to observe the dog's behavior. People living alone would report that they had never seen their dog do this because no one was available to witness the behavior. He also suggests that in some households people might not be very observant of what the dog was

doing and might not even notice that the dog was sitting by the front door. Another of his suggestions is that some dogs might be less sensitive to their person than others, either through having a relationship that wasn't that great or lacking the perception that other dogs might have.

Sheldrake went on to do a series of experiments with a dog named Jaytee and his person Pam, in England. Initially, Pam kept a log of when she was going to come home, and Jaytee's activity was monitored by Pam's parents. Later, Sheldrake videotaped Jaytee's activity with a time-stamp that was cross-checked with the time that Pam started to come home. Pam varied the time that she started for home, and came home sometimes in her own car and sometimes in a taxi. This was done to try to eliminate the possibility that Jaytee had simply learned Pam's routine and would go to the door just by knowing what time Pam usually came home, and also to eliminate the possibility that Jaytee learned to associate the sound of Pam's car and used extraordinary hearing to detect Pam's car at a great distance.

The results of these experiments showed that regardless of what time Pam chose to come home, and regardless of whether she came home in her own car or a taxi, Jaytee would go and sit by the door some ten minutes before Pam arrived.

The bottom line is that, despite humans having lived with dogs for some fifty thousand years, we still know very little about their abilities. We make assumptions about them, but these assumptions are often limited by our shortsightedness and lack of imagination.

10

HOW TO TALK TO YOUR DOG

To talk to your dog, you must first study and learn dog language. Go through the chapters on body language, growling, and barking, and make sure you know what all of the signals mean. Study them well and observe your dog carefully to notice what your dog does in different contexts.

This is going to take some time. Let's do a thought experiment. Let's say that you were transplanted to a village in France where no one spoke any English and you didn't speak any French. You could do one of several things. You could raise your voice and say words in English louder, assuming that the louder you speak the more chance there is that the villagers will understand you. You could start to pay attention to the signs that the villagers give you with their hands and body language while they are speaking French. You could start trying to repeat some words in French, trying to learn the context in which these words are spoken. In the first case you will never communicate successfully with anyone. In the second and third cases you will gradually learn how to communicate with the people in the village.

Don't expect instant results. Talking to your dog is a matter of observation and trial and error on your part. If you're a quick study, you'll be able to talk to your dog sooner rather than later. If you're not a quick study, you will eventually learn how to talk to your dog, but like learning to communicate in any language, it takes time and effort.

You have to commit to the time and effort.

At first, it might be frustrating, because it might seem that you can't really see any of the signals that are described in the previous chapters. But over time, your observational skills will sharpen and you will see the more subtle things like the ears moving around or the pupil of the eye widening. That's how all languages are learned. We first go through a period of having a hard time understanding just the basics, and then over time, we start to learn more and more of the subtleties of the language. With time, effort, and application, we eventually become fluent in the language.

I want you to become fluent in dog language.

No, I don't mean learning to bark, whine, move your ears, or wag your tail. I mean starting to get a sense of what your dog is feeling, wanting, or fearing. I mean learning their visual and vocal cues so that you can understand your dog better.

That understanding can lead to knowing what situations and actions are going to lead to what response behaviors in your dog and changing or adjusting your signals and behaviors to ones that your dog will more easily understand and respond to.

This doesn't mean that eventually you can have philosophical discussions with dogs about the meaning of life.

This does mean that you will be able to understand what the dog is trying to tell you and be able to convey to your dog what you want your dog to understand.

Let's get started on how to do this.

First, as I mentioned already, you need to study thoroughly all of the previous chapters and make sure that you understand everything that was being said.

Second, you need to keep in mind that just as with people, dog language is multimodal. That means that either the same signal is sent by different body parts or the different body parts act together to modify the meaning of the signal. Think of what happens when you talk to someone. Your facial expression changes as you talk. The inflection of your voice changes. You can move your head from side to side. You can slump down to make yourself look smaller or raise yourself up to make yourself look taller. You can wave your hands and arms around to emphasize different points. All of that plays a role in conveying the message that you're trying to get across to your listener.

It's the same with dogs. In conveying a message, a dog might wag her tail, lift up her body posture, move her head to the side, change

the position of the eyes, change the size of the pupils, open or close her mouth, move her ears, and bark or whine. All of that can convey a message, just like our spoken sentence conveys a message.

You may think, how will I ever keep all of this straight?

The answer is, one step at a time.

Choose one body part (ears or tail are good starting points) and pay attention to what happens to that body part in different contexts. Over time you will learn how that body part responds in different situations as the dog is trying to get across a message to you or someone around you.

Once you have mastered the meaning of one body part, choose another one. Repeat the process of paying attention to the different contexts in which that body part is used to signal messages.

Step by step, go through all of the different body parts and associate their changes with different contexts. The dog wants to go for a walk? What is the tail doing? The dog wants to eat? What is the tail doing? The dog sees a strange dog? What is the tail doing? Someone rings the doorbell? What is the tail doing?

This works best if you keep a journal where the entries are the date, the context, and the behavior of this specific part that you are observing. For example:

March 23, 2023, dog is fed chicken, tail is wagging vigorously more to the right than to the left.

March 24, 2023, dog is fed liver, tail is wagging slowly and more to the left than the right.

March 25, 2023, the kids come to visit and bring over their dog. Dog's tail is wagging slowly and more to the left.

March 26, 2023, friend comes over to visit and brings her dog who loves to play with dog. Dog's tail is wagging vigorously and more to the right than to the left.

What is your guess about how your dog feels in each of those situations?

The reason that I suggest including the date is that this will give you a sense of how you progress over time in learning the meaning of the different signals of your dog. You will be able to see day by day how much more you can identify of the signals of each body part that you study.

Once you become fluent in dog language, it is time for you to start talking to your dog.

As I mentioned previously, dogs are pretty good at learning human languages, specifically words that you speak in different contexts. You can continue talking to your dog and there is a great chance that your dog will understand much of what you say.

But you can modify your spoken words with body language and tonal quality that your dog will understand.

Let's take a look at some situations where you can do this.

Your dog is frightened, anxious, or upset. Sit down next to him. Sitting is a calming signal. If your dog is still frightened, yawn multiple times. Yawning is another calming signal. Do not tower over your dog, leaning above him. Give him some space and look at him from a sitting position.

You want your dog to pay attention to what you are saying. Tilt your head to one side. Make the expression on your face animated, smiling, changing. Dogs stop paying attention to people whose facial expression doesn't change.

You want to praise your dog for doing something you like. Tell him in a high-pitched voice, as high as you can get your voice to go. High-pitched vocalizations are seen as approval from a pack member. You can say something like "Good dog!" in a high-pitched voice.

Don't hug your dog while you are doing this. Some dogs don't like to be hugged.

You want to stop your dog from doing something that you don't like. Tell him in a low-pitched voice, as low as your voice can go. Low-pitched vocalizations are seen as warning growls. You can say something like "No!" sharply in a low-pitched voice. Don't put your hand on top of the dog's head or muzzle while you are saying this. In the context of a reprimand, a dog could view that as a threat.

You want your dog to respond in a happy manner. Don't interact with your dog when you are anxious or upset. The dog will pick up on this and also become anxious and upset. Put on a happy face, smiling and laughing.

You want your dog to greet you when you come home after a long day. Walk in and make happy noises, laughing, waving your arms around, maybe throwing a ball. Call your dog and greet him with a smiling face.

Your dog growls at you when you want to touch or move his food dish. Change your feeding behavior. Put your dog on a sit-stay while you put the dish down, and then tell your dog okay and let him start eating. If he refuses to behave, temporarily take away or withhold his food dish. This shows your dog that you, and not he, control access to resources.

Your dog pushes past you to go through a door. Put her on a sit-stay while you walk through the door, and then tell her okay to let her go through the door after you. This teaches your dog that you have priority of where you go. This is especially important when you're leaving your car. A dog who has not learned to wait until his person gives the release command to get out of the car is a dog whose life is in danger because he might well jump out into oncoming traffic.

Your dog shows you that she is scared of something. Identify what that something is and remove it from the dog's environment. It might be anything. A picture, a statue, a houseplant, a toy that makes noise. Remove it or hide it away. Your dog will thank you.

Your dog shows you that he feels territorial and aggressive when someone comes to the door. Put your dog on a sit-stay, perhaps even using a leash, raise yourself to your full height, and in a confident voice say, "I am in charge and I am handling this situation." Or simply say, "I've got this."

Your dog shows you that she likes interacting with a certain dog. Schedule play dates with that dog.

Your dog shows you that she hates being with a certain dog. Don't invite that dog over to your house.

Your dog shows you that he is afraid of being left alone. Do several things. First, leave the house or apartment for short periods of time, say five minutes, then return and watch the body language of your dog. He will typically greet you. If he doesn't, it could mean that something in the house is scaring him. Determine what that is and remove it. Then leave for longer periods, say thirty minutes, and come back. Gradually extend the time that you are away. You can play music for your dog while you are gone. Classical music has been shown to be quite soothing for dogs.

Talking to dogs is a two-way street. On the one hand, you are learning what your dog is trying to tell you. On the other hand, you are conveying to the dog what is important to you.

With time, as you learn more of the subtleties of dog language and your dog learns more of the subtleties of your language, you can start having pleasant conversations.

11

MENTAL COMMUNICATION

You should now be fluent in dog language. As you watch and learn about your dog and what she likes and dislikes, you'll gradually gain a lot of insight into what your dog is thinking and what she is trying to communicate to you. By watching your dog's body language, you can assess her mood and her level of motivation. All of what you have learned so far about dog signals has been shown experimentally and has been validated scientifically.

If you are content with that and do not want to stretch your mind into areas that science has not tested, then it's best that you stop right here. You have all of the scientifically approved tools to understand your dog's body signals, and dogs can usually understand much of human language, at a simple level at least, so you can talk to your dog in language and read from the dog's body language what the dog is trying to convey to you.

However, if you are willing to venture into lands that science has not approved, then read on.

Because the next step is to mentally communicate with your dog.

My introduction to this was when I was offering training lessons to people and their dogs. At the time, more than fifteen years ago, some trainers used force to break a dog's spirit and compel her to act the way the trainer desired. There was a lot of yanking of leashes, pulling the dog around, pushing the dog down, and even swinging the dog through the air by the collar. This was done all in the name of dominating the dog and making her do things when she had no clue what was desired of her.

I thought that I could do better by showing respect for the dog. I didn't allow any physical force to be used. Praise was used liberally, said in a high-pitched voice that dogs find reassuring, and corrections were in the form of a sharply worded "No" in a low-pitched voice. While some trainers use treats as rewards for desired behavior, I preferred using people's voices. Dogs quickly learn to do what is expected of them while the treats are flowing, but once the treats are gone, they often refuse to do anything. Treats get depleted, but voices—and the love and approval of people—are always there.

The first behavior that I taught to my classes was to get the dog to sit. I would have people say "Sit" and point to the ground with the index finger of their hand. Some dogs caught on immediately while others looked at their people with great confusion. The dogs that immediately sat were instantly rewarded with their person saying, "Good dog!" Other dogs who didn't respond would walk around for a while, get tired, and finally sit, at which point they too would be rewarded with "Good dog!"

The problem with this approach was that it would take some dogs quite a while to get to the point where they would sit. While most dogs in the class were already sitting, other dogs would walk around endlessly until they became tired and finally sat. As you can imagine, this was pretty boring for most people and their dogs, waiting for every dog in the class to finally sit.

Because I had such variable responses from dogs, I wanted to find out what might have caused this variation. Were some dogs naturally more obedient? Were some dogs smarter? Were some dogs more easily distracted? Were some dogs just stubborn? To find out, I asked a lot of people about their dogs and about how they felt when they were giving their dogs the "Sit" command. Asking about how smart their dogs were was a nonstarter. Everyone thought that they had smart dogs. Opinions about the other questions were all over the map.

However, finally, one detail emerged that really surprised me. The people whose dogs responded quickly said that they visualized their dog sitting and had a clear picture of the dog in a sitting position while they gave the "Sit" command. Following up on this with people whose dogs didn't catch on too quickly, they said that they were thinking about a variety of different things as they instructed their dog to sit—what to

have for dinner, when would the class ever end, what to pick up from the store on the way home, what great shoes the person next to them was wearing . . .

This led me to try an experiment with one of my classes. I told everyone to visualize their dog in a sitting position as they gave the command and to try to keep that image as clear as possible in their mind.

Surprisingly, it worked!

Not all dogs responded quickly, but they all responded quicker than in previous classes where I did not ask anyone to visualize anything. When I asked the people whose dogs responded more slowly, they confessed that they had trouble visualizing their dogs and couldn't keep a clear image in their minds.

Subsequently, I used the visualization technique to teach people and their dogs other, more complex commands: "Down," with a hand sweeping down toward the ground and visualizing the dog lying down; "Wait," with a hand making a chopping motion in front of the dog, signifying that the dog is supposed to wait for a short time, with a visualization of the dog staying in one position for a few moments and then doing something else; "Stay," with a hand motion blocking the

dog's face, signifying that the dog must stay in one place until another command is given, with a corresponding visualization; "Come," with a hand movement toward the person's chest, signifying that the dog is supposed to come to the person, and the visualization that the dog is running or trotting up to their human; and "Heel," with a hand motion slapping the left hip and a visualization of the dog trotting alongside the person.

As a scientist, I found all of this to be surprising. Nowhere in the scientific journals that I routinely read did anyone speak of visualization as something that dogs could perceive.

I set out to expand my quest for information more broadly and found that there was a lot of anecdotal information about dogs and people communicating mentally. These were not the controlled experiments that I was used to. Instead these were anecdotes of what people observed in their interactions with dogs and other animals.

Here's what they said.

The first step is to build a mental bridge between you and your dog that allows you to mentally communicate with each other.

The concept of a mental bridge comes from J. Allen Boone's book *Kinship with All Life*. In the book, Boone describes his life with a German shepherd named Strongheart, who was a canine movie star in the fledgling Hollywood movie industry of the 1920s. Strongheart was born in 1917 in Germany. During World War I he was trained as a police dog and served in the German Red Cross. In 1920, Strongheart was brought to the United States, where he was purchased by Laurence Trimble, a movie director. Trimble worked with Strongheart and made him into the first canine movie star in the United States. Although Strongheart was initially aggressive and suspicious of everyone, following his training as a police dog, Trimble worked with him and made him trust people.

Boone was asked to take care of Strongheart when Trimble had to go away for a while. Knowing nothing about dogs, Boone started out assuming that Strongheart was not very smart, because he was just a dog. However, Strongheart quickly showed Boone his intelligence, and they went on to have a variety of adventures, during which Boone learned to mentally communicate with the dog. He freely admits in the book that his views of animals changed during this time, and he credits Strongheart as being his teacher.

Boone's advice is to start by changing your attitude. Stop looking at the dog as an inferior creature, a dumb brute who is not capable of thinking. Stop characterizing you as a superior human and the dog as stupid.

Look at both you and your dog as equals, as fellow creatures that inhabit this planet, each with thoughts, hopes, and dreams of their own.

At first, this is going to be very hard. Our education, our social contacts with other people, and our books stress that animals are inferior, animals don't think, and animals don't have language. Creeping into our social discourse is the realization that dogs have feelings, but we see these as unimportant compared to our feelings, which we see as complex and difficult to understand.

As a scientist, much of my education emphasized that dogs, as well as other animals, operated on programs of instinct, hardwired into them by their genetics. To think otherwise was considered a sin, an act of anthropomorphism, which means ascribing human behaviors to animals. A complete no-no.

I remember being at a conference of animal behaviorists, where a person was presenting the results of his research to an audience of about one hundred fellow scientists. As he was talking about the reproductive behavior of a species of bird, he said: the female bird wants to have more babies. Immediately, a hand shot up into the air from the audience. The presenter stopped and let the hand-raiser speak, who said: do you mean that natural selection made the bird try to have more babies, even though the bird doesn't have any conscious desire to do so? The presenter backtracked and said, yes, the bird is programmed through natural selection to make it seem like she wants to have more babies. The audience collectively breathed a sigh of relief—anthropomorphism was averted.

Much of dog training involves getting the dog to do what we want. We train our dogs to sit, to lie down, to heel, without considering what the dogs want or need. Whether this is done through brute force or through a gentle system of rewards for desired behavior, this is still a form of dominating our dogs. With this mind-set we place the dog in an inferior position, subject to our whims or our convenience. There is little thought of the convenience of the dog because of our view that dogs are our property and are somewhat dim-witted, so we need to teach them how to behave around us.

And yes, dogs do need to learn how to behave around us.

But learning how to behave around us doesn't mean that dogs should be treated as inferior beings.

The way to build a bridge of mental communication with your dog is to start with a journal where you jot down every behavior that you observe in your dog and try to guess the motivation for that behavior.

Adopt a positive attitude toward every motivation rather than a negative one. Your dog pees on your favorite rug. No, the dog doesn't hate you and isn't trying to make your life miserable. What could be going on in your dog's life that might make him do that? Maybe there is a bladder infection. Maybe the rug smells particularly unpleasant to the

dog. Maybe you don't notice when the dog has to go outside to pee, and the dog is finally left with the choice of having his bladder burst or peeing on the rug. Look at the possible motivations with a positive spin.

Compiling a list of behaviors and their possible motivations does two things for you. One is that you are much more attuned to what your dog is doing, and the other is that you start freeing yourself from negative judgments about your dog.

All animals respond to kindness, affection, love, and positive feelings. You are well on your way to building a mental bridge once you can always look at your dog in this way.

Kindness, affection, love, and positive feelings go a long way toward connecting with all animals, and not just dogs.

Let me give you an example. I live in the high desert, where there are a lot of rattlesnakes. My neighbors consider them dangerous, and they certainly can be, particularly if someone is trying to kill or capture them. But I look at rattlesnakes with positive feelings.

One day I was walking to the back door of my house when I noticed a three-foot-long diamondback rattlesnake on the back porch. I had just come out of that door moments before, so the snake must have been in the weeds a few feet or perhaps even inches from where I walked. She was quite calm, exploring the porch and pushing on the

door with her head. I walked up to within about ten feet, admiring the beauty of this magnificent animal. She kept on exploring, and then slowly started to move off the porch into the surrounding weeds. Then she changed her mind and came back to the porch, which is level with the ground and covers a crawl space that extends under the house. Finding a knot-sized hole in one of the porch boards, she first stuck about a foot of her body into the hole, then emerged to look at me for a few moments, and then slowly slid entirely through the knot hole, out of sight and under the house.

She made no attempt to coil up, no attempt to rattle, no attempt to attack me. We mutually acknowledged each other, and we went our separate ways. My neighbors kill rattlesnakes when they find them, and the snakes are aggressive and defend themselves. But here there was no aggression. Only perhaps mutual respect.

The snake took up living under the porch. On warm days, she would come out through the knot hole and sun herself, stretching out her full length across the wooden slats of the porch. On more than one occasion, I would come out of the back door, forgetting to look for her, and step within a couple of feet of her head or her tail. She would lazily rattle once or twice, in effect saying, hey stupid, I'm here, don't step on me. I would mentally apologize, go back into the house, and go out the front door to give her space. Eventually, I saw that she was probably pregnant, and I didn't want a lot of baby rattlesnakes running around, so I had a friend move her to a safe habitat in the desert.

But don't get me wrong. I respect, and even admire, these creatures, but I don't assume they're not dangerous. Even though that snake was used to my scent and may have viewed me as a "fellow resident," I still am careful to avoid appearing to threaten them or accidentally stepping on them, because then I know there's a good chance I'll get bitten.

Once you have established feelings of love, appreciation, and kindness toward your dog, you can begin trying to mentally communicate.

Find a place where you can sit with your dog, where you will not be disturbed. Put away phones and other distractions. Turn off any music. You want to be in complete stillness, just you and your dog.

Accept that your dog can hear your thoughts. The challenge for you is to listen to your dog's thoughts.

Visualization is the key.

Ask your dog a question, either out loud or just thinking about it. Keep it simple. Most dogs are pretty good at understanding our language. If the question is something that you can visualize, do so and keep the image in your mind for a few seconds. My reading of Temple Grandin's book *Thinking in Pictures* has shown me that it's likely that animals think in pictures, so if you can make a picture in your mind about your question, that's a good place to start.

Look at your dog and try to sense an answer to your question. The answer will come as a picture or a sense of knowing, as if you are making a guess. At first, the connection will be very faint, and you might think that you are imagining things. Don't let a sense of skepticism prevail.

Accept what comes to you, even if you think that it is a guess or you think that your mind is playing tricks on you. Doubt is the enemy of communication.

Practice this on a daily basis, maybe ten to fifteen minutes per day. Your mind will get tired if you do this for more than that initially, and you will start feeling that nothing is working, and it's silly to think that you can talk to your dog in this way.

Gradually, over several weeks, you will start feeling that you are indeed getting something from your dog.

That is the time for validation.

Ask your dog some questions that you don't know the answers to. Maybe where she hid her favorite bone. Maybe where she last peed in the yard. Maybe where she last pooped when you weren't watching.

Then go and check. Did you get the right answer?

If you didn't, keep at it. Eventually, the answers will come, and they will allow you to build up your confidence that this is all real, and not some trick of your imagination.

If you did, congratulations. You are on your way to talking mentally with your dog.

ACKNOWLEDGMENTS

I want to thank all of the people and dogs who contributed to my learning about dog language. This includes clients who consulted with me about the behavioral problems of their dogs, people who participated in the dog training classes that I offered, and people who asked me a variety of questions about dog behavior. I also want to thank my wife, Dr. Judith Kiriazis, for her insights into the behavior of dogs and her extensive comments about this manuscript. A gifted teacher, she was an integral part of the dog training program and helped come up with ways of explaining concepts and movements that made sense to the dogs' people. I also thank Laura Wood of Fine Print Literary Agency, my agent, who was always there for me, answering questions and communicating with publishers, particularly when I was writing *Chasing Doctor Dolittle*. I thank my editor, Eugene Brissie of Lyons Press, for working with me and for selecting all of the photographs that are in this book. Finally, I want to thank all of my dogs—Nenkin, Beowulf, Little Fly, Little Monkey, Raja, and Zephyr—for being the best teachers of dog behavior that I possibly could have had. Sadly, none of them is with me now. It is the tragedy of dog-human relationships that dogs live such short lives, leaving people to mourn them forever.

SOURCES AND
FURTHER READING

CHAPTER 1. DOGS HAVE LANGUAGE

Andrews, E. F., R. Pascalau, A. Horowitz, G. M. Lawrence, and P. J. Johnson. 2022. "Extensive Connections of the Canine Olfactory Pathway Revealed by Tractography and Dissection." *The Journal of Neuroscience* 42 (33): 6392–407.

Bekoff, M. 2023. *Dogs Demystified*. Novato, CA: New World Library.

Bensky, Miles K., Samuel D. Gosling, and David L. Sinn. 2013. "The World from a Dog's Point of View: A Review and Synthesis of Dog Cognition Research." *Advances in the Study of Behavior* 45: 209–406.

Coren, S. 2000. *How to Speak Dog*. New York: The Free Press.

Demirbas, Y. S., H. Ozturk, B. Emre, M. Kockaya, T. Ozvardar, and A. Scott. 2016. "Adults' Ability to Interpret Canine Body Language during a Dog-Child Interaction." *Anthrozoos* 29 (4): 581–96. doi: 10.1080/08927936.2016.1228750.

Dror, S., A. Miklosi, A. Sommese, A. Temesi, and C. Fugazza. 2021. "Acquisition and Long-Term Memory of Object Names in a Sample of Gifted Word Learner Dogs." *R Soc Open Sci* 8 (10): 210976. doi: 10.1098/rsos.210976.

Fraser, M. M. 2019. "Dog Words—or, How to Think without Language." *Sociological Review* 67 (2): 374–90. doi: 10.1177/0038026119830911.

Gabor, A., M. Gacsi, D. Szabo, A. Miklosi, E. Kubinyi, and A. Andics. 2020. "Multilevel fMRI Adaptation for Spoken Word Processing in the Awake Dog Brain." *Sci Rep* 10 (1): 11968. doi: 10.1038/s41598-020-68821-6.

Kaminski, J., J. Call, and J. Fischer. 2004. "Word Learning in a Domestic Dog: Evidence for 'Fast Mapping.'" *Science* 304: 1682–83.

Mariti, Chiara, Angelo Gazzano, Jane Lansdown Moore, Paolo Baragli, Laura Chelli, and Claudio Sighieri. 2012. "Perception of Dogs' Stress by

Their Owners." *Journal of Veterinary Behavior* 7 (4): 213–19. doi: 10.1016/j .jveb.2011.09.004.

Meints, K., V. Brelsford, and T. De Keuster. 2018. "Teaching Children and Parents to Understand Dog Signaling." *Frontiers in Veterinary Science* 5. doi: 10.3389/fvets.2018.00257.

Myers-Schulz, B., M. Pujara, R. C. Wolf, and M. Koenigs. 2013. "Inherent Emotional Quality of Human Speech Sounds." *Cognition & Emotion* 27 (6): 1105–113. doi: 10.1080/02699931.2012.754739.

Nose, Izuru, and Miki Kakinuma. 2019. "Japanese Version of the Dog Personality Scale: Reliability and Validity Based on Owner and Dog Instructor Evaluation and Behavioral Observation." *Applied Animal Behaviour Science* 214: 72–78. doi: 10.1016/j.applanim.2019.03.008.

Overall, Karen L. 2018. "Animals Tell Us How They Get Information, What Matters to Them and What Disturbs Them: We Simply Need Listen." *Journal of Veterinary Behavior* 27: v–vi. doi: 10.1016/j.jveb.2018.08.004.

Parsons, C. E., R. T. LeBeau, M. L. Kringelbach, and K. S. Young. 2019. "Pawsitively Sad: Pet-Owners Are More Sensitive to Negative Emotion in Animal Distress Vocalizations." *R Soc Open Sci* 6 (8): 181555. doi: 10.1098 /rsos.181555.

Slobodchikoff, C. N. 2012. *Chasing Doctor Dolittle: Learning the Language of Animals.* New York: St. Martin's Press.

Tami, G., and A. Gallagher. 2009. "Description of the Behaviour of Domestic Dog (*Canis familiaris*) by Experienced and Inexperienced People." *Applied Animal Behaviour Science* 120 (3–4): 159–69. doi: 10.1016/j.ap planim.2009.06.009.

Virányi, Zsófia, and Friederike Range. 2014. "On the Way to a Better Understanding of Dog Domestication." In J. Kaminski and S. Marshall-Pescinii, eds. *The Social Dog* (pp. 35-62) New York: Academic Press.

Wan, M., N. Bolger, and F. A. Champagne. 2012. "Human Perception of Fear in Dogs Varies According to Experience with Dogs." *PLoS One* 7 (12): e51775. doi: 10.1371/journal.pone.0051775.

CHAPTER 3. HOW TO READ YOUR DOG

Bekoff, M., and J. Pierce. 2009. *Wild Justice: The Moral Lives of Animals.* Chicago: University of Chicago Press.

Demirbas, Y. S., H. Ozturk, B. Emre, M. Kockaya, T. Ozvardar, and A. Scott. 2016. "Adults' Ability to Interpret Canine Body Language during a Dog-Child Interaction." *Anthrozoos* 29 (4): 581–96. doi: 10.1080/0892 7936.2016.1228750.

Ferres, Kim, Timo Schloesser, and Peter A. Gloor. 2022. "Predicting Dog Emotions Based on Posture Analysis Using DeepLabCut." *Future Internet* 14 (4). doi: 10.3390/fi14040097.

Horowitz, A., and J. Hecht. 2016. "Examining Dog-Human Play: The Characteristics, Affect, and Vocalizations of a Unique Interspecific Interaction." *Anim Cogn* 19 (4): 779–88. doi: 10.1007/s10071-016-0976-3.

Kundey, S. M. A., A. De los Reyes, E. Royer, S. Molina, B. Monnier, R. German, and A. Coshun. 2011. "Reputation-like Inference in Domestic Dogs (*Canis familiaris*)." *Anim Cogn* 14: 291–302.

Leaver, S. D. A., and T. E. Reimchen. 2008. "Behavioural Responses of Canis familiaris to Different Tail Lengths of a Remotely-Controlled Life-Sized Dog Replica." *Behaviour* 145: 377–90.

Mariti, Chiara, Caterina Falaschi, Marcella Zilocchi, Jaume Fatjó, Claudio Sighieri, Asahi Ogi, and Angelo Gazzano. 2017. "Analysis of the Intraspecific Visual Communication in the Domestic Dog (*Canis familiaris*): A Pilot Study on the Case of Calming Signals." *Journal of Veterinary Behavior* 18: 49–55. doi: 10.1016/j.jveb.2016.12.009.

Marshall-Pescini, S., C. Passalacqua, A. Ferrario, P. Valsecchi, and E. Prato-Previde. 2011. "Social Eavesdropping in the Domestic Dog." *Animal Behaviour* 81 (6): 1177–83.

Mellor, D. J. 2018. "Tail Docking of Canine Puppies: Reassessment of the Tail's Role in Communication, the Acute Pain Caused by Docking and Interpretation of Behavioural Responses." *Animals* 8 (6). doi: 10.3390 /ani8060082.

Quaranta, A., M. Siniscalchi, and G. Vallortigara. 2007. "Asymmetric Tail-Wagging Responses by Dogs to Different Emotive Stimuli." *Curr Biol* 17 (6): R199–201. doi: 10.1016/j.cub.2007.02.008.

Range, F., L. Horn, Z. Viranyi, and L. Huber. 2009. "The Absence of Reward Induces Inequity Aversion in Dogs." *PNAS* 106: 340–45.

Rugaas, T. 2005. *On Talking Terms with Dogs: Calming Signals.* Direct Book Service.

Siniscalchi, M., R. Lusito, G. Vallortigara, and A. Quaranta. 2013. "Seeing Left- or Right-Asymmetric Tail Wagging Produces Different Emotional Responses in Dogs." *Curr Biol* 23 (22): 2279–82. doi: 10.1016/j .cub.2013.09.027.

Sommese, A., A. Miklosi, A. Pogany, A. Temesi, S. Dror, and C. Fugazza. 2022. "An Exploratory Analysis of Head-Tilting in Dogs." *Anim Cogn* 25 (3): 701–5. doi: 10.1007/s10071-021-01571-8.

Tami, G., and A. Gallagher. 2009. "Description of the Behaviour of Domestic Dog (*Canis familiaris*) by Experienced and Inexperienced People." *Applied Animal Behaviour Science* 120 (3–4): 159–69. doi: 10.1016/j.ap planim.2009.06.009.

CHAPTER 4. FACES

Bloom, T., and H. Friedman. 2013. "Classifying Dogs' (*Canis familiaris*) Facial Expressions from Photographs." *Behav Processes* 96: 1–10. doi: 10.1016/j .beproc.2013.02.010.
Bremhorst, A., D. S. Mills, L. Stolzlechner, H. Wurbel, and S. Riemer. 2021. "'Puppy Dog Eyes' Are Associated with Eye Movements, Not Communication." *Front Psychol* 12: 568935. doi: 10.3389/fpsyg.2021.568935.
Burza, L. B., T. Bloom, P. H. E. Trindade, H. Friedman, and E. Otta. 2022. "Reading Emotions in Dogs' Eyes and Faces." *Behav Processes* 202: 104752.
Call, J., J. Brauer, J. Kaminski, and M. Tomasello. 2003. "Domestic Dogs (*Canis familiaris*) Are Sensitive to the Attentional State of Humans." *J Comp Psychol* 117 (3): 257–63. doi: 10.1037/0735-7036.117.3.257.
Murata, K., M. Nagasawa, T. Onaka, N. Kanemaki, S. Nakamura, K. Tsubota, K. Mogi, and T. Kikusui. 2022. "Increase of Tear Volume in Dogs after Reunion with Owners Is Mediated by Oxytocin." *Curr Biol* 32 (16): R869–70. doi: 10.1016/j.cub.2022.07.031.
Racca, A., E. Amadei, S. Ligout, K. Guo, K. Meints, and D. Mills. 2009. "Discrimination of Human and Dog Faces and Inversion Responses in Domestic Dogs (*Canis familiaris*)." *Anim Cogn* 13: 525–33. doi: 10.1007 /s10071-009-0303-3.
Teglas, E., A. Gergely, K. Kupan, A. Miklosi, and J. Topal. 2012. "Dogs' Gaze Following Is Tuned to Human Communicative Signals." *Curr Biol* 22 (3): 209–12. doi: 10.1016/j.cub.2011.12.018.

CHAPTER 5. DOGS BARKING AND GROWLING

Balint, A., T. Farago, A. Miklosi, and P. Pongracz. 2016. "Threat-Level-Dependent Manipulation of Signaled Body Size: Dog Growls' Indexical Cues Depend on the Different Levels of Potential Danger." *Anim Cogn* 19 (6): 1115–31. doi: 10.1007/s10071-016-1019-9.

Deaux, E. C., J. A. Clarke, and I. Charrier. 2015. "Aggressive Bimodal Communication in Domestic Dogs, *Canis familiaris*." *PLoS One* 10 (11): e0142975. doi: 10.1371/journal.pone.0142975.

Epperlein, T., G. Kovacs, L. S. Ona, F. Amici, and J. Brauer. 2022. "Context and Prediction Matter for the Interpretation of Social Interactions across Species." *PLoS One*.

Farago, T., P. Pongracz, A. Miklosi, L. Huber, Z. Viranyi, and F. Range. 2010. "Dogs' Expectation about Signalers' Body Size by Virtue of Their Growls." *PLoS One* 5 (12): e15175. doi: 10.1371/journal.pone.0015175.

Faragó, Tamás, Péter Pongrácz, Friederike Range, Zsófia Virányi, and Ádám Miklósi. 2010. "'The bone is mine': Affective and Referential Aspects of Dog Growls." *Animal Behaviour* 79 (4): 917–25. doi: 10.1016/j.anbehav.2010.01.005.

Lehoczki, Fanni, Zsuzsa Szamosvölgyi, Ádám Miklósi, and Tamás Faragó. 2019. "Dogs' Sensitivity to Strange Pup Separation Calls: Pitch Instability Increases Attention Regardless of Sex and Experience." *Animal Behaviour* 153: 115–29. doi: 10.1016/j.anbehav.2019.05.010.

Manser, Marta B. 2010. "The Generation of Functionally Referential and Motivational Vocal Signals in Mammals." I*Handbook of Mammalian Vocalization—An Integrative Neuroscience Approach* 19: 477–86.

Maros, K., P. Pongrácz, G. Bárdos, C. Molnár, T. Faragó, and A. Miklósi. 2008. "Dogs Can Discriminate Barks from Different Situations." *Applied Animal Behaviour Science* 114 (1–2): 159–67.

Maskeliunas, R., V. Raudonis, and R. Damasevicius. 2018. "Recognition of Emotional Vocalizations of Canine." *Acta Acustica* 104: 304–14.

Molnar, C., P. Pongracz, T. Farago, A. Doka, and A. Miklosi. 2009. "Dogs Discriminate between Barks: The Effect of Context and Identity of the Caller." *Behav Processes* 82 (2): 198–201.

Molnar, C., F. Kaplan, P. Roy, F. Pachet, P. Pongracz, A. Doka, and A. Miklosi. 2008. "Classification of Dog Barks: A Machine Learning Approach." *Anim Cogn* 11 (3): 389–400. doi: 10.1007/s10071-007-0129-9.

CHAPTER 6. DOGS AND A SENSE OF SMELL

Andrews, E. F., R. Pascalau, A. Horowitz, G. M. Lawrence, and P. J. Johnson. 2022. "Extensive Connections of the Canine Olfactory Pathway Revealed by Tractography and Dissection." *The Journal of Neuroscience* 42 (33): 6392–407.

Carlone, Beatrice, Angelo Gazzano, Jara Gutiérrez, Claudio Sighieri, and Chiara Mariti. 2018. "The Effects of Green Odour on Domestic Dogs: A Pilot Study." *Applied Animal Behaviour Science* 207: 73–78. doi: 10.1016/j .applanim.2018.06.005.

Dorrigiv, I., M. Hadian, and M. Behram. 2023. "Comparison of Volatile Compounds of Anal Sac Secretions between the Sexes of Domestic Dog (*Canis lupus familiaris*)." *Vet Res Forum* 14 (3): 169–76. doi: 10.30466/vrf .2023.1983063.3714.

Horowitz, A. 2016. *Being a Dog*. New York: Scribner.

CHAPTER 7. DOG TRAINING

Blackwell, E. J., C. Twells, A. Seawright, and R. A. Casey. 2008. "The Relationship between Training Methods and the Occurrence of Behavior Problems, as Reported by Owners, in a Population of Domestic Dogs." *Journal of Veterinary Behavior* 3 (5): 2017–217.

Cracknell, N. R., D. S. Mills, and P. Kaulfuss. 2008. "Can Stimulus Enhancement Explain the Apparent Success of the Model-Rival Technique in the Domestic Dog (*Canis familiaris*)?" *Applied Animal Behaviour Science* 114: 461–72.

Herron, M. E., F. S. Shofer, and I. R. Reisner. 2009. "Survey of the Use and Outcome of Confrontational and Non-Confrontational Training Methods in Client-Owned Dogs Showing Undesirable Behaviors." *Applied Animal Behaviour Science* 117: 47–54.

McKinley, S., and R. J. Young. 2003. "The Efficacy of the Model-Rival Method When Compared with Operant Conditioning for Training Domestic Dogs to Perform a Retrieval-Selection Task." *Applied Animal Behaviour Science* 81: 357–65.

Turcsán, Borbála, Enikő Kubinyi, and Ádám Miklósi. 2011. "Trainability and Boldness Traits Differ between Dog Breed Clusters Based on Conventional Breed Categories and Genetic Relatedness." *Applied Animal Behaviour Science* 132 (1–2): 61–70. doi: 10.1016/j.applanim.2011.03.006.

Westgarth, Carri, Robert M. Christley, Gina L. Pinchbeck, Rosalind M. Gaskell, Susan Dawson, and John W. S. Bradshaw. 2010. "Dog Behaviour on Walks and the Effect of Use of the Leash." *Applied Animal Behaviour Science* 125 (1–2): 38–46. doi: 10.1016/j.applanim.2010.03.007.

CHAPTER 8. DOG EMOTIONS

Albuquerque, N., K. Guo, A. Wilkinson, B. Resende, and D. S. Mills. 2018. "Mouth-Licking by Dogs as a Response to Emotional Stimuli." *Behav Processes* 146: 42–45. doi: 10.1016/j.beproc.2017.11.006.

Albuquerque, N., K. Guo, A. Wilkinson, C. Savalli, E. Otta, and D. Mills. 2016. "Dogs Recognize Dog and Human Emotions." *Biol Lett* 12 (1): 20150883. doi: 10.1098/rsbl.2015.0883.

Bekoff, M. 2007. *The Emotional Lives of Animals.* Novato, CA: New World Library.

Blackwell, Emily J., John W. S. Bradshaw, and Rachel A. Casey. 2013. "Fear Responses to Noises in Domestic Dogs: Prevalence, Risk Factors and Co-Occurrence with Other Fear Related Behaviour." *Applied Animal Behaviour Science* 145 (1–2): 15–25. doi: 10.1016/j.applanim.2012.12.004.

Burza, L. B., T. Bloom, P. H. E. Trindade, H. Friedman, and E. Otta. 2022. "Reading Emotions in Dogs' Eyes and Faces." *Behav Processes* 202: 104752.

Casey, R. A., M. Naj-Oleari, S. Campbell, M. Mendl, and E. J. Blackwell. 2021. "Dogs Are More Pessimistic If Their Owners Use Two or More Aversive Training Methods." *Sci Rep* 11 (1): 19023. doi: 10.1038/s41598-021-97743-0.

Doring, D., A. Roscher, F. Scheipl, H. Kuchenhoff, and M. H. Erhard. 2009. "Fear-Related Behaviour of Dogs in Veterinary Practice." *Veterinary Journal* 182 (1): 38–43. doi: 10.1016/j.tvjl.2008.05.006.

Dzik, V., C. Cavalli, M. Iglesias, and M. Bentosela. 2019. "Do Dogs Experience Frustration? New Contributions on Successive Negative Contrast in Domestic Dogs (*Canis familiaris*)." *Behav Processes* 162: 14–19. doi: 10.1016/j.beproc.2019.01.007.

Ferres, Kim, Timo Schloesser, and Peter A. Gloor. 2022. "Predicting Dog Emotions Based on Posture Analysis Using DeepLabCut." *Future Internet* 14 (4). doi: 10.3390/fi14040097.

Flint, Hannah E., Jason B. Coe, David L. Pearl, James A. Serpell, and Lee Niel. 2018. "Effect of Training for Dog Fear Identification on Dog Owner Ratings of Fear in Familiar and Unfamiliar Dogs." *Applied Animal Behaviour Science* 208: 66–74. doi: 10.1016/j.applanim.2018.08.002.

Kundey, S. M. A., A. De los Reyes, E. Royer, S. Molina, B. Monnier, R. German, and A. Coshun. 2011. "Reputation-like Inference in Domestic Dogs (*Canis familiaris*)." *Anim Cogn* 14: 291–302.

Lenkei, R., S. Alvarez Gomez, and P. Pongracz. 2018. "Fear vs. Frustration—Possible Factors behind Canine Separation Related Behaviour." *Behav Processes* 157: 115–24. doi: 10.1016/j.beproc.2018.08.002.

Racca, A., E. Amadei, S. Ligout, K. Guo, K. Meints, and D. Mills. 2009. "Discrimination of Human and Dog Faces and Inversion Responses in Domestic Dogs *(Canis familiaris)*." *Anim Cogn* 13: 525–33. doi: 10.1007 /s10071-009-0303-3.

Scheumann, M., A. S. Hasting, S. A. Kotz, and E. Zimmermann. 2014. "The Voice of Emotion across Species: How Do Human Listeners Recognize Animals' Affective States?" *PloS One* 9 (3): e91192. doi: 10.1371/journal .pone.0091192.

Scheumann, M., A. S. Hasting, E. Zimmermann, and S. A. Kotz. 2017. "Human Novelty Response to Emotional Animal Vocalizations: Effects of Phylogeny and Familiarity." *Front Behav Neurosci* 11: 204. doi: 10.3389 /fnbeh.2017.00204.

CHAPTER 9. THINGS WE DON'T KNOW ABOUT DOGS

Benediktova, K., J. Adamkova, J. Svoboda, M. S. Painter, L. Bartos, P. Novakova, L. Vynikalova, V. Hart, J. Phillips, and H. Burda. 2020. "Magnetic Alignment Enhances Homing Efficiency of Hunting Dogs." *Elife* 9. doi: 10.7554/eLife.55080.

Duranton, Charlotte, Thierry Bedossa, and Florence Gaunet. 2016. "When Facing an Unfamiliar Person, Pet Dogs Present Social Referencing Based on Their Owners' Direction of Movement Alone." *Animal Behaviour* 113: 147–56. doi: 10.1016/j.anbehav.2016.01.004.

Feuerstein, N., and J. Terkel. 2008. "Interrelationships of Dogs *(Canis familiaris)* and Cats *(Felis catus L.)* Living under the Same Roof." *Applied Animal Behaviour Science* 113 (1–3): 150–65. doi: 10.1016/j.applanim.2007.10.010.

González-Ramírez, Mónica Teresa, Minerva Vanegas-Farfano, and René Landero-Hernández. 2018. "Differences in Stress and Happiness between Owners Who Perceive Their Dogs as Well Behaved or Poorly Behaved When They Are Left Alone." *Journal of Veterinary Behavior* 28: 1–5. doi: 10.1016/j.jveb.2018.07.010.

Jackson-Grossblat, Amy, Nancy Carbonell, and Dennis Waite. 2014. "The Therapeutic Effects upon Dog Owners Who Interact with Their Dogs in a Mindful Way." *Journal of Humanistic Psychology* 56 (2): 144–70. doi: 10.1177/0022167814559390.

Piotti, Patrizia, Rebecca Marie Spooner, Hoi-Lam Jim, and Juliane Kaminski. 2017. "Who to Ask for Help? Do Dogs Form an Opinion on Humans Based on Skilfulness?" *Applied Animal Behaviour Science* 195: 93–102. doi: 10.1016/j.applanim.2017.05.024.

Range, F., A. Kassis, M. Taborsky, M. Boada, and S. Marshall-Pescini. 2019. "Wolves and Dogs Recruit Human Partners in the Cooperative String-Pulling Task." *Sci Rep* 9 (1): 17591. doi: 10.1038/s41598-019-53632-1.

Sheldrake, R. 1999. *Dogs That Know When Their Owners Are Coming Home.* New York: Three Rivers Press.

CHAPTER 10. HOW TO TALK TO YOUR DOG

Gabor, A., M. Gacsi, D. Szabo, A. Miklosi, E. Kubinyi, and A. Andics. 2020. "Multilevel fMRI Adaptation for Spoken Word Processing in the Awake Dog Brain." *Sci Rep* 10 (1): 11968. doi: 10.1038/s41598-020-68821-6.

Mills, D. S. 2005. "What's in a Word? A Review of the Attributes of a Command Affecting the Performance of Pet Dogs." *Anthrozoos* 18 (3): 208–21. doi: 10.2752/089279305785594108.

Ramos, Daniela, and Daniel S. Mills. 2019. "Limitations in the Learning of Verbal Content by Dogs during the Training of OBJECT and ACTION Commands." *Journal of Veterinary Behavior* 31: 92–99. doi: 10.1016/j.jveb.2019.03.011.

Ratcliffe, V. F., and D. Reby. 2014. "Orienting Asymmetries in Dogs' Responses to Different Communicatory Components of Human Speech." *Curr Biol* 24 (24): 2908–12. doi: 10.1016/j.cub.2014.10.030.

CHAPTER 11. MENTAL COMMUNICATION

Boone, J. A. 1954. *Kinship with All Life.* San Francisco: Harper & Row.

Boone, J. A. 2013. *Adventures in Kinship with All Life.* Joshua Tree, CA: Tree of Life Books.

Grandin, T. 2008. *Thinking in Pictures.* New York: Vintage.

INDEX

ABOUT THE AUTHOR

Con Slobodchikoff is an animal behaviorist who has a PhD from the University of California, Berkeley. He is a professor emeritus of biology at Northern Arizona University, where he taught courses in animal behavior and did research on the communication system and social biology of prairie dogs. He is also the CEO of Animal Communications, Ltd., which has worked with people and their pets by providing dog training classes and counseling about pet behaviors, and the founder and chief science officer of Zoolingua, which is building a dog translator using artificial intelligence technology.

Con is the author of *Chasing Doctor Dolittle: Learning the Language of Animals*, which presents evidence that a number of animals either have their own languages or have language-like abilities, and is the lead author of *Prairie Dogs: Communication and Community in an Animal Society*, which summarizes what we know about prairie dogs, including the groundbreaking work of Con and his team in decoding prairie dog language. He has also edited three other books on ecology and behavior and has published around one hundred works on behavior, evolution, and conservation biology.

Con's work has been featured widely in the media. His video appearances have included The Future of Dogs, Dateline NBC, ABC World News, CNN, Country Canada, Quantum (Australian Broadcasting Corporation), Teirzeit (Belgian-German TV), BBC, Turner Broadcasting, Brixen Productions (Discovery Channel), and Evolve (History Channel). His work was the subject of two one-hour documentaries, *Talk of the Town* (BBC) and *Prairie Dog Chatter* (Animal Planet Wild Kingdom).

He has also been interviewed on various radio outlets, including Trailblazers with Walter Isaacson, The Diane Rehm Show, Radio Lab, NPR's All Things Considered, NPR's Morning Edition, and BBC radio. Stories about his work have appeared in the *LA Times, Boston Globe, Denver Post, Washington Post, New York Times*, and others, as well as numerous magazines including *Smithsonian Magazine, National Geographic, People Magazine*, and *Discover Magazine.*

When he is not studying animals, Con enjoys photography. His work can be found at the website www.artabstractphotography.com and on Instagram @artabstractphotography.

To find out more about Con, see his website, www.conslobod chikoff.com.